Education
for
Positive
Mental Health

norc

NATIONAL OPINION RESEARCH CENTER
MONOGRAPHS IN SOCIAL RESEARCH

Education for Positive Mental Health

*A Review
of Existing Research
and Recommendations
for Future Studies*

By

JAMES A. DAVIS

ALDINE PUBLISHING COMPANY
Chicago

616.807
D294

The research reported herein was supported by a grant from Pennsylvania Mental Health, Inc.

*First published 1965 by
ALDINE Publishing Company
320 West Adams Street
Chicago, Illinois 60606*

*Library of Congress Catalog Card Number 64–15607
Designed by Greer Allen
Printed in the United States of America*

Preface

One of the signs that a field of inquiry is reaching a stage of maturity is the appearance of a rash of self-criticism and intellectual stock-taking. The field of mental health research, which, under the generous support of the National Institute of Mental Health, has seen an enormous growth since World War II, has begun to show signs of having reached such a stage. The nine volumes of the Joint Commission on Mental Health and Illness represent the largest, although by no means the final, effort in this campaign.

One of the organizations which has been prominent in activities that contribute to constructive criticism in the field of mental health is Pennsylvania Mental Health, Inc., a voluntary, non-profit, statewide citizens' organization devoted to public education in the field of mental health. This organization is affiliated with the National Association for Mental Health and is financed primarily by divisions of the Community Chest and United Fund of Pennsylvania. Its major purposes are twofold. Its first is to conduct programs of public education as to the nature and extent of mental illness, and methods of treating it, and to mobilize citizens for action to improve the care and treatment of the mentally ill. Its second purpose is to conduct programs of public education aimed at raising the level of the community's mental health; that is, to teach the application of the principles of preventive psychiatry.

Since its founding, Pennsylvania Mental Health, Inc., has conducted an outstandingly successful series of campaigns to improve the care of the mentally ill, and its staff has felt this aspect of its program to be on a sound footing. In the second area of its program, education for positive mental health, a number of concerns have arisen. These concerns stem, not from the belief that many educational programs founded by the organization were failures, but from the fact that these programs did not rest on the basis of fully documented principles and that they were not subjected to research evaluation.

In 1958, Pennsylvania Mental Health, Inc., along with the American Psychiatric Association and the National Association for Mental Health, sponsored a two-and-one-half-day "National Assembly on Mental Health Education." At this meeting a distinguished group of experts, including, among others, Carl Binger, Francis Braceland, Orville Brim, Jr., John Clausen, Elaine Cumming, Erik Erikson, Eric Lindemann, Ralph Ojemann, Lloyd Rowland, and William Foote Whyte, discussed the problem of conducting mental health education programs. The experts disagreed on many points, and none could indicate substantial, technically adequate research findings to provide a justification or direction for mental health education activities. The results of the conference are summarized in *Mental Health Education: A Critique* (Pennsylvania Mental Health, Inc., 1960).

In 1962 Max Silverstein, executive director of Pennsylvania Mental Health, Inc., approached NORC with the suggestion that we conduct a review of the published research literature on positive mental health and develop proposals for studies that would help answer the questions raised at the Assembly. Dr. James A. Davis of NORC's staff undertook this task. This monograph is the result of his efforts to develop a program for mental health education that is based on the best available empirical data and contains his recommendations for evaluation studies of the program which would enable an organization sponsoring such a program to tell whether the program is successful.

Attempts to inaugurate programs of mental health education have been plagued with numerous difficulties. There is no generally accepted definition of mental health. Thus it is not clear what the subject matter of such an educational program would be. There is no consensus about what principles underlie the achievement of a state of mental health. Thus it is difficult to know the best method of presentation. Indeed, there is not even agreement on the identity of the major variables that influence mental health, nor is there consensus about the ways in which the variables considered important should be studied or about the proper ways to measure such variables. While there are many theories — some of them conflicting, some of them simply approaching the phenomenon from such diverse points of view that it is impossible to tell whether they conflict or complement one another — almost all of them share the characteristic that they have very little empirical support.

To anyone familiar with the scope of the literature in the area of mental health, the magnitude of the task Dr. Davis has undertaken will be apparent. What is not apparent, however, particularly to those who are concerned with the fact that a great number of studies in the field leave much to be desired from the technical point of view, and the fact that few studies appear to be concerned with populations of sufficient size to have any degree of generality, is the surprisingly large number of technically competent and generalizable studies that Dr. Davis has turned up.

In this fuzzy, contradictory, and chaotic forest of studies, Dr. Davis has wielded his ax and cleared the underbrush to reveal the genuine trees. Starting from the simplest possible set of assumptions about the nature of mental health, and utilizing a reasonably "hard," although not unrealistically perfectionistic, set of criteria for the scientific adequacy of studies, Dr. Davis outlines the variables that have the greatest degree of acceptance as important for mental health. From there he proceeds to show what we have in fact found out about these variables and their interrelationships, setting forth clearly the conclusions that can be drawn from these studies. He then outlines recommendations for the course of future research in those areas in which conclusions are currently rather shaky.

This book is much more than a traditional review of the literature and recommendations for further study. It is a significant contribution toward clarifying and codifying the major findings of mental health research for which there are sound empirical data and toward formulating a theoretical viewpoint which gives meaning and guidance to the establishment of a mental health education program. Dr. Davis has gone far beyond the critical summary of existing findings and has brought together, reanalyzed, and in some instances, when the data were available, provided additional analyses. He has taken such pains in order to make as nearly comparable as possible a range of studies that, although drawn from diverse sources and samples, are shown to have a remarkable degree of consistency of findings. There thus emerges from this study a set of solidly established generalizations, providing a foundation on which to build a more detailed and comprehensive knowledge of the dynamics of mental health. Dr. Davis is able to show that, in fact, we know more than the skeptics thought we knew, although we are still far short of the level of knowledge that some of the more exuberant researchers in the field of mental health like to think we have attained.

In this book, Dr. Davis has performed a valuable service for all who labor in the area of mental health research. He has brought together in one volume and in a clear and concise manner the important substantive findings of the field. But he has also laid out a blueprint for further research in the area of educational programs that may change mental health in a population, providing a framework that should enrich and make continually more meaningful the course of mental health's research in the future.

NORMAN M. BRADBURN
Acting Director
National Opinion Research Center

Contents

List
of
Tables

List of Tables

List of Tables

1

Introduction

Because this study was written by a social scientist who is not a specialist in the area of mental health,[1] and because it concerns an entity (positive mental health) which is undefinable and possibly non-existent, it requires a longer introduction than its bulk would otherwise warrant. The author was commissioned to review the literature in the field of mental health, with a view to developing a proposal for a mental health education program based on the best available knowledge in the field, and to undertake an evaluation study that would demonstrate the efficacy of the program. I was given a free hand to proceed as I thought best in order to accomplish these very broad aims.

In grappling with this unusual commission, we began, and wisely I think, by deciding not to attempt to define mental health. Offhand such a decision appears cavalier and illogical, but it seems justified by the meager results of previous attempts. Even Jahoda's (1958) outstanding work does not yield a definition suitably unambiguous to translate into research operations.

Instead, we bagan by searching the published research literature for studies concerning positive mental health, loosely circumscribed as follows.

A study was included if (1) it was judged to be free of gross deficiencies in design and analysis, (2) it was based on a population whose members were not undergoing treatment by a psy-

---

[1] The author holds a Ph.D. degree in sociology and is currently Associate Professor of Sociology at the University of Chicago and a Senior Study Director at NORC. His field of specialization is in survey research techniques, and his professional leaning is toward "hard" (statistical, operational, experimental) rather than "soft" (clinical, case study, participant observation) research. His only previous contact with the study of mental health took place a number of years ago when he was a member of a research team in Boston studying the post-hospital adjustment of schizophrenics.

chiatrist or clinical psychologist, and (3) it presented data on (*a*) subjective reports of worries, nervousness, psychosomatic symptoms, happiness, etc., (*b*) ratings of adjustment or mental health by social scientists or psychiatrists, or (*c*) knowledge or acceptance of "principles" of psychodynamics, psychopathology, or development, other than college-level courses in the behavioral sciences.

No one of these phenomena can be justified as the best measure of "positive mental health," but together they encompass the great bulk of the research and writing in the field. Only very broad definitions (e.g., "self-fulfillment," "maturity," "maximum effectiveness," etc.) were excluded.

Although, on the basis of casual knowledge and the reading of some hortatory essays in the field, I had assumed that the existing leterature was essentially useless and the proposed studies could start from scratch, this proved not to be the case. It is true that the vast bulk of the studies published have been of such low technical quality—in terms of representative samples, controls, measurement, and statistical analysis—that they are literally worse than useless, but there remain a surprisingly large number of excellent studies, both experimental and cross-sectional. For instance, without even pretending to attempt thorough coverage, it was possible to locate close to twenty reasonably well-executed evaluation studies.

This is not to say that the findings were consistent, that there were not huge gaps, or that research knowledge was firm enough to justify the educational projects now operating. It was clear, however, that any proposed research must take the existing findings into consideration, and no available publication provides an adequate review of these materials. Before turning to the proposed research, therefore, we shall review the existing knowledge.

Our work was unavoidably superficial because of my lack of expertise and the broad scope of the field (a recent bibliography compiled by Kelly [1962] cites 1,158 items). Almost no work done outside the United States was covered, the entire search was conducted in about a month, and studies excluded by our criteria for narrowness of definition were ignored. The most important limiting factor was our decision to exclude all studies that were technically deficient. Because so much of the research on mental health is barely suggestive, much less persuasive, this criterion cut a considerable swath through the references, and a number of familiar titles are not included in the bibliographies. Such a decision involved a considerable degree of subjective judgment, and we do not claim methodological infallibility. However, most of the exclusions were for simple and obvious defects — experiments done without control groups, samples with N's so small that they preclude statistical analysis, contrasts between populations which obviously differ on many variables other than the one in question, publications which do not present any data at all. If anything, we erred on the side of generosity.

In sum, a review of the remaining technically satisfactory literature turned up so many studies that it was necessary to consider their findings before proposing new research. Chapters 2, 3, and 4 are devoted to this task, and to conclusions and recommendations. Chapters 2 and 3 treat non-experimental research on the major variables and their relationships, and Chapter 4 reviews a number of experimental attempts to modify mental health phenomena in normal populations.

In organizing the materials, we found it useful to think of mental health education as a set of programs based on the following assumptions about human behavior and development.

1. Mental health
   a) We assume that in the general population of adults there is a state, or set of closely related states, which can be called "mental health."
   b) We assume that there is quantitative variation in mental health — some people are well adjusted, some people are poorly adjusted, and, at the extreme, some people are mentally ill.
2. Principles of mental health
   a) We assume that specific principles can be stated regarding cause-and-effect relationships in mental health, particularly regarding:
   (1) Techniques of emotional adjustment for adults.

    (2) Principles of emotional development in children.

  b) We assume that the acceptance of these principles leads to improved mental health:

    (1) Directly through improved adjustment.

    (2) Indirectly through improved emotional development in children.

3. Non-intellectual factors

  a) We assume that mental health in adults is affected by current environmental situations ("stresses").

  b) At the same time, we assume that past experiences, particularly childhood development, have a permanent effect on mental health and susceptibility to mental illness.

We can also express these ideas in the accompanying diagram.

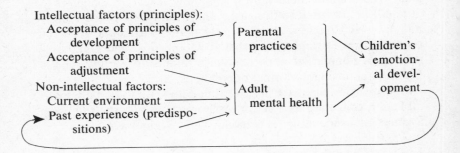

If correct, these ideas provide a powerful argument for mental health education, particularly since the circularity of the process (indicated by the arrow from "Children's emotional development" back to "Past experiences") means that changes introduced into the system have cumulative effects. We assume that attempting to improve mental health in adults by teaching them mental health principles or by manipulating their environment will have positive effects, not only on the target population, but on future generations.

Because these ideas are very abstract and do not specify the variables involved (e.g., what mental health principles, what aspects of the current environment, what parental practices) the scheme is not really a theory. Rather, it serves to organize the mass of potentially relevant materials. Thus we can use the scheme to organize Chapters 2 and 3 around the following questions.

1. The major variables
   a) Adult mental health
      (1) Is it reasonable to think of adult mental health as a single dimension?
      (2) Is it reasonable to assume that mental illness is at the extreme end of a continuum of states of mental health?
   b) Principles of mental health
      (1) What principles are endorsed by the general population and the experts?
      (2) How do population groups vary in accepting these principles?
   c) Principles of child development
      (1) What principles are endorsed by the general population and the experts?
      (2) How do population groups vary in accepting these principles?
2. Relations among the variables
   a) Adult mental health
      (1) What is known about relationships between the mental health of adults and their acceptance of principles of mental health?
      (2) What is known about environmental correlates of adult mental health?
      (3) What is known about past experiences and mental health?
   b) Children's emotional development
      (1) What is known about parental practices and their children's emotional development?
      (2) What is known about the mental health of parents and their children?

2
Existing Knowledge: The Major Variables

ADULT MENTAL HEALTH

The nature of mental health in adult, non-clinical populations is, naturally, the single most important research area to be reviewed. In this chapter we review a number of studies which have attempted to measure mental health through behavioral-science research techniques. First we examine the question of dimensionality—whether it is justifiable to consider mental health as an entity—and then we discuss the problem of degrees of mental health.

The Problem of Dimensionality

The assessment of mental health in normal populations presents tremendous problems, both technical and substantive. Perhaps the most important problem is whether to consider mental health a single phenomenon or a tent covering a wide variety of separate and distinct entities. Conceptually or theoretically, the issue is very difficult to approach, much less to resolve. However, in considering research data, it can be translated into a clear statistical problem—the degree of correlation between alternative measures. Ideally, one would proceed as follows: (1) list all possible definitions of mental health, (2) devise a measure for each, (3) administer all the measures to a large representative sample, and (4) compute the intercorrelations among the measures. Forgetting, for the moment, technical problems of statistics and measurement, we can say that if one finds strong positive intercorrelations, then mental health may be considered a single entity, in the sense that highly correlated measures may be assumed to be tapping the same source. But if correlations are zero, one would have to conclude that there are independent dimensions of mental health and deal with these dimensions. Negative correlations, of course, would suggest something like alternative manifestations of some underlying disease which was endemic.

Our results, naturally, will by no means be that clear-cut, but by reviewing a number of studies involving multiple measurement of mental health, we may draw some generalizations. We shall consider, first, measures based on subjects' self-descriptions, and then, more briefly, agreement among expert ratings of mental health in normal populations.

Subjective measures. — The relationships among various subjective (self-rating) measures of mental health are particularly important, because a case can be made for their face validity. That is, while a person who thinks he has a heart condition may or may not really have one, anyone who thinks he is unhappy or worried or nervous really is unhappy or worried or nervous. In contrast to physical illness and some psychoses (although it is my impression that a high proportion of psychotics believe they are mentally ill), when we consider mental health in the general population, the symptom is the disease.

Although we paid little attention to the many studies intercorrelating or subjecting to factor analysis items in various personality scales for small and unrepresentative populations, the five studies listed below reported intercorrelations for a considerable number of items on large and reasonably representative samples.

1. Shirley A. Star's studies on military personnel in World War II (Star, 1949*a*, *b*).
2. *Americans View Their Mental Health,* a recent national survey conducted by the University of Michigan Survey Research Center (Gurin, Veroff, and Feld, 1960).
3. Unpublished NORC data on a national sample of arts and science graduate students (Davis, 1962).

4. Unpublished data from *The Housing Environment and Family Life* (Wilner *et al.*, 1962).
5. Fred Fiedler's survey of college students and soldiers (Fiedler *et al.*, 1958).

A landmark series of researches conducted during World War II has been reported in a four-volume series entitled *Studies in Social Psychology in World War II*, commonly (and hereinafter) referred to as *The American Soldier*. We will treat numerous findings from these studies, but at present we are concerned with data from the chapter by Star (1949*b*) reporting the development of the Neuropsychiatric Screening Adjunct (NSA), a questionnaire designed to detect inductees whose mental health was questionable enough to warrant interviews by psychiatrists.

In order to develop the instrument, the research workers collected a battery of over one hundred items by means of self-administered questionnaires from, first, 3,501 white enlisted men with no overseas experience and, second, 563 psychoneurotic patients in army hospitals. The author constructed Guttman scales (a technique for combining items which, according to particular statistical criteria, tap a single dimension) for fifteen specific areas. Seven of the scales treat the soldiers' reports of current complaints and problems; the other eight refer to childhood and pre-army situations. The seven measures, and sample items from them, are given below.

1. "Psychosomatic Symptoms": Health problems, trouble getting to sleep or staying asleep, spells of dizziness, nervousness, sick headaches, "cold sweats," etc.
2. "Personal Adjustment": What sort of time do you have in the army? In general, how would you say you feel most of the time—in good spirits or in low spirits? Do you think you can make good in the army?
3. "Acceptance of Soldier Role": If it were up to you, and you yourself had to decide, would you choose to be a soldier or a civilian? What kind of an outfit would you rather be in —combat overseas, non-combat overseas, or an outfit that will stay in the U.S.?
4. "Oversensitivity": Do you often say things you wish later

you hadn't said? How often do people hurt your feelings? Do you ever feel like smashing things for no good reason?

5. "Worry": Do you worry very much about things that might happen to you? Do you ever seriously worry about whether or not there will be a real depression after this war?

6. "Sociability": How would you say the people you know feel about you? (Almost all of them like me, most of them like me, etc.) Before you came into the army did you usually go around with a bunch of others or by yourself?

7. "Identification with the War Effort": In your opinion is the United States fighting for things that you feel are worth fighting for? Do you think you have as much of a personal stake in this war as anybody else?

Except for psychosomatic symptoms, each of the groups formed a satisfactory Guttman scale, which indicates high internal correlations (internal correlations, however, are not reported in the book). Table 2.1 shows the product-moment correlations among the seven scales in the 3,501-case army cross-section[1] (correlations among the psychoneurotic are almost identical) and the correlation between the scale and the distinction—cross-section versus psychoneurotic (Star, 1949*b*, pp. 32, 496, 497).

Each of the correlations is positive, although not all are strong. Since a correlation of .081 is significant at the .01 level, for samples of 1,002 or more we may assume that all the coefficients are reliable, even though the sample is undoubtedly heavily clustered. Soldiers who are low on a given index of mental health or adjustment are disproportionately likely to be low on other measures, and low scores on each questionnaire scale help to distinguish between the army cross-section and the hospitalized psychoneurotics. Some of the correlations are "obvious" (e.g., the .35 correlation between acceptance of the role of soldier and identification with the war effort), but it is less obvious that identification with the war effort should be related to psychosomatic symptoms. Similarly, the fact that

---

[1] A study method in which the subjects under observation are contacted only once.

Table 2.1 Product-Moment Correlations among Mental Health Measures in *The American Soldier*

Scales	Personal Adjustment	Symptoms	Soldier Role	Worry	Oversensitivity	War Effort	Sociability
Personal adjustment		.50	.49	.41	.43	.32	.17
Symptoms			.46	.43	.37	.23	.19
Soldier role				.35	.22	.35	.15
Worry					.34	.23	.15
Oversensitivity						.25	.22
War effort							.23
Sociability							
Cross-section versus psychoneurotics	.42	.66	.35	.27	.33	.12	.33

symptoms and personal adjustment show the highest correlation (.50) in the table may surprise those who believe that somatic symptoms tend to be a substitute for conscious distress.

The data were subjected to factor analysis, from which the author concluded, first, that no more than one dimension could be profitably extracted and, second, that the psychosomatic-symptoms index was the best single measure of the underlying dimension. While the absolute size of the relationships in many instances warns us that they cannot be considered interchangeable, the structure of the intercorrelations supports the idea of unidimensionality.

The most recent and most representative sample in mental health studies is the 1957 national probability sample of personal interviews conducted by the University of Michigan's Survey Research Center and reported by Gurin, Veroff, and Feld (1960) in their study entitled *Americans View Their Mental Health*. In terms of sampling, questionnaire design, interviewing, and coverage (American adults, twenty-one or older, living in private households) the study meets the highest standards of survey research. Because the research was conducted on a tight time schedule in order to meet the needs of the Joint Commission on Mental Illness and Health, the analysis has a number of gaps. However, the volume provides a rich source of materials, and subsequent analyses of the data are continuing at the Survey Research Center.

We shall draw on data from the book, and also from a recent article by the same authors (Veroff, Feld, and Gurin, 1962) in examining the problem of intercorrelating subjective measures.

In *Americans View Their Mental Health* intercorrelations are reported only for items in a twenty-item symptom check-list (trouble sleeping, nervousness, upset stomach, health trouble, etc.) very similar to the psychosomatic-symptoms index in *The American Soldier*. A matrix of intercorrelations is given separately for 956 men (p. 179) and 1,221 women (p. 180). The only other intercorrelation reported is a cross-tabulation (p. 29) of the questions, "Taking things altogether, how would you say things are these days — would you say you're very happy, pretty happy, or not too happy these days?" ("Happiness") and, "Do you worry about things a lot or not very much?" ("Worry"). Our calculations give a fairly low Q value of .166 for these two items, which are very roughly comparable to the "Personal Adjustment" and "Worry" scales in *The American Soldier*.

Veroff, Feld, and Gurin (1962) factored the symptom matrices and identified four different but intercorrelated factors, getting similar results for men and women. The four symptom factors and the items chosen by Veroff, Feld, and Gurin as their measures are as follows.

1. "Physical Health"
   a) Do you feel you are bothered by all sorts of pains and ailments in different parts of your body?
   b) For the most part, do you feel healthy enough to carry out the things you would like to do?
2. "Physical Anxiety"
   a) Have you ever been bothered by shortness of breath when you were not exercising or working hard?
   b) Have you ever been bothered by your heart's beating hard?
3. "Psychological Anxiety"
   a) Do you ever have any trouble getting to sleep or staying asleep?
   b) Have you ever been bothered by nervousness, feeling fidgety and tense?
4. "Immobilization"
   a) Do you find it difficult to get up in the morning?
   b) Are you troubled by your hands' sweating so that you feel damp and clammy?

Intercorrelations between scores on indices based on the above questions are reproduced in Table 2.2, values in the white area being for 1,036 men and values in the shaded area for 1,332 women (Gurin, Veroff, and Feld, 1960, p. 185).

The correlations are significant and positive, but they are low, and the matrix has a different structure from that in Table 2.1. Here, each measure is more closely related to its immediate neighbor than to more distant measures, so that, at the extremes, immobilization and physical health have a barely significant correlation.

In a recent article, the Survey Research Center team has expanded the analysis on two subsamples from its survey: 255 employed married men with children and 542 married women with children. The items mentioned above (the four symptom factors, "Worry," and "Happiness") along with a variety of additional measures ("Inadequacy as a Parent," "Lack of Uniqueness," "Marital Happiness," etc.) were given factor analyses separately for each sex. By and large, the results for men and women were very similar, although particular items load differently in the two sexes. Considering only items with similar loadings for both sexes, the resulting factors and sample items are the following.

1. "Felt Psychological Disturbance" (symptoms)
   Items loading on this factor are the four symptom factor scores, except that for men "Physical Health" loads on a separate dimension.
2. "Unhappiness"
   a) "Happiness," as defined above.
   b) "Marital Happiness": Taking all things together, how would you describe your marriage—very happy, a little happier than average, just about average, or not too happy?
3. "Social Inadequacy"
   a) "Job Problems" (applied only to men in these analyses): Have you ever had any problems with your work—times

Table 2.2 Intercorrelations of Symptom Factor Indices in *Americans View Their Mental Health**

Symptom Factor Indices	Physical Health	Physical Anxiety	Psychological Anxiety	Immobilization
Physical health		.38	.27	.08
Physical anxiety	.38		.39	.19
Psychological anxiety	.32	.39		.29
Immobilization	.12	.22	.24	

* Shaded area indicates women (N = 1,332), white area indicates men (N = 1,036).

when you couldn't work or weren't getting along on the job, or didn't know what kind of work you wanted to do?

b) "Marital Inadequacy": Many men (women) feel that they're not as good husbands (wives) as they would like to be. Have you ever felt this way?

c) "Parental Inadequacy": Many men (women) feel that they're not as good fathers (mothers) as they would like to be. Have you ever felt this way?

d) "Shortcomings in the Self": If you had a son (daughter) how would you like him (her) to be different from you? (Wants child to be different.)

4. "Lack of Identity"

a) "Lack of Uniqueness": What are some of the ways in which you're different from most other people? (Sees no difference.)

b) "Lack of Strong Points in the Self": What would you say were your strongest points? (Sees none.)

Another way of viewing the results is to rearrange the matrices of zero-order correlations so that variables are grouped according to their factor loadings. We do this in Table 2.3, the values in the white area being for the male sample and the values in the shaded area for the female. Parentheses around a coefficient indicate that it is not statistically significant at the .01 probability level.

Because there are 169 coefficients in the table, we can draw a wide variety of conclusions. For the moment, let us merely note the following.

1. Of the total number of relationships, one is significantly negative (between "Worry" and "Ill Health" for men), eighty-seven are not significant at the .01 level, and eighty-one (48 per cent of the total) are significant and positive.

2. "Worry," "Lack of Uniqueness," "Lack of Strong Points," and "Shortcomings in the Self" are essentially independent of the other items.

3. The symptom indices, "Happiness," "Marital Happiness," "Marital Inadequacy," and "Parental Inadequacy" tend to

Table 2.3 Tau Beta Intercorrelations (*Americans View Their Mental Health*), Decimals Omitted*

	Felt Psychological Disturbance					Unhappiness		Social Inadequacy				Lack of Identity		Not Loaded on Any
	Physical Health (1)	Physical Anxiety (2)	Psychological Anxiety (3)	Immobilization (4)	Total Symptoms (5)	Happiness (6)	Marital Happiness (7)	Marital Inadequacy (8)	Parental Inadequacy (9)	Job Problems (10)	Shortcomings in the Self (11)	Lack of Uniqueness (12)	Lack of Strong Points (13)	Worry (14)
1		32	16	11	36	14	12	(−01)	(06)	11	(−02)	(−02)	(03)	−17
2	25		32	27	58	12	11	(10)	17	15	(05)	(05)	(06)	(−07)
3	24	32		34	57	16	13	20	15	12	(06)	(−04)	(02)	(01)
4	(07)	25	23		41	12	(04)	24	14	16	(09)	−11	(01)	(09)
5	38	58	58	33		24	15	20	23	22	(09)	(00)	(03)	(00)
6	10	15	19	(02)	18		38	15	(08)	(03)	(10)	(07)	(04)	19
7	(06)	18	15	(01)	20	44		(04)	(00)	(01)	14	(05)	18	13
8	(00)	14	15	16	16	(−01)	(01)		30	26	15	(02)	11	(10)
9	(00)	13	16	15	16	(03)	(04)	37		25	18	(−08)	11	(07)
10	†	†	†	†	†	†	†	†	†		13	(02)	(−06)	(08)
11	(−03)	(07)	(08)	14	(08)	(00)	(04)	20	16	†		(−07)	(06)	18
12	(00)	(−04)	(−06)	(−01)	(−03)	(02)	(02)	(−01)	(04)	†	(−05)		11	(−04)
13	(07)	(03)	(01)	(−04)	(−01)	(04)	(04)	(01)	(−01)	†	(−03)	13		(−01)
14	(06)	(08)	19	(06)	14	18	(05)	(08)	(04)	†	(05)	(−04)	(−01)	

*Shaded area indicates 542 married women with children; white area, 225 employed married men with children. Numbers in parentheses – (<.11) for men, (<.10) for women – are not significant at the .01 level. Numbering in headings and at side is from the item list in *The American Soldier*.

†Not applicable to women.

show low positive relationships, but nineteen out of seventy-two (26 per cent) of their associations are not significant.

There is a sharp contrast between the results in *The American Soldier* and those in *Americans View Their Mental Health*. Even though both studies apply similar measures to rather large and heterogeneous samples, both conduct similar analyses, and both demonstrate a high level of technical competence, they lead to opposite conclusions about the important question of uni-dimensionality. Part of this discrepancy may be due to technical problems: the questions in the two studies are not identical; one matrix is based on scales and the other on individual items; the measures of association are different; the sample sizes are very different. However, the items on symptoms provide a set

American Soldier	Americans View Their Mental Health
1. Do you have any particular physical or health problem?	20. Identical.
2. Do you often have trouble getting to sleep or staying asleep?	1. Identical.
3. Do your hands ever tremble enough to bother you?	14. Identical.
5. Are you ever bothered by nervousness?	2. Have you ever been bothered by nervousness, feeling fidgety or tense?
6. Have you ever been bothered by your heart's beating hard?	9. Identical.
8. Have you ever had spells of dizziness?	11. Identical.
10. Have you ever been bothered by shortness of breath when you were not exercising or working hard?	8. Identical.
11. Are you ever troubled by your hands' sweating so that they feel damp and clammy?	15. Are you troubled by your hands' sweating so that you feel damp and clammy?
12. Are you ever troubled with sick headaches?	3. Are you ever troubled by headache or pains in the head?
13. How often are you bothered by having an upset stomach?	5. Identical.
14. Are you ever bothered by having nightmares (dreams that frighten or upset you very much)?	12. Are you ever bothered by nightmares?

of materials in which practically identical single questions were asked. The accompanying list shows the items which are identical or almost identical in the two studies.

The agreement is close enough that a confrontation of the two studies on these items can avoid the problems of different question-wording and scales versus single items. Since *Americans View Their Mental Health* reports a matrix of correlations for 956 men (p. 179), and *The American Soldier* reports a matrix of cross-tabulations for 3,501 men (pp. 540–43), the sample sizes are roughly comparable, and sex is held constant.

Table 2.4 shows the product-moment correlations from *Americans View Their Mental Health* in the white area and product-moment correlations computed for this report from *The American Soldier* data in the shaded area. (Numbering is from the item list in *The American Soldier*.) Since the mean value in *Americans View Their Mental Health* is .257, and the mean for the *American Soldier* data is .247, we can say that, when the two studies ask identical questions, there is little difference in the levels of correlations reported.

More important, however, is the fact that there is a fair agree-

Table 2.4 Product-Moment Correlations from *Americans View Their Mental Health* and *The American Soldier**

The American Soldier	Americans View Their Mental Health										
	1	2	3	5	6	8	10	11	12	13	14
1. Health problems		24	20	25	26	29	36	11	22	20	12
2. Sleep	24		28	51	24	26	28	16	28	22	23
3. Hands tremble	20	32		39	27	26	27	37	22	19	26
5. Nervousness	31	39	49		34	34	32	36	34	28	26
6. Heart beating hard	19	20	19	30		36	52	20	17	27	20
8. Dizziness	16	30	19	27	31		36	18	32	22	27
10. Shortness of breath	14	16	19	25	26	25		21	19	17	10
11. Hands clammy	21	25	29	36	26	19	22		20	16	21
12. Headaches	18	27	18	30	16	34	17	20		27	20
13. Upset stomach	20	30	22	32	18	24	20	27	26		19
14. Nightmares	08	30	28	30	25	27	27	26	23	28	

*Shaded area indicates correlations for *The American Soldier*; white area, for *Americans View Their Mental Health*. Average correlation (N = 55): *The American Soldier*, .247; *Americans View Their Mental Health*, .257. Numbering from item list in *The American Soldier*.

ment between the two studies in the sizes of particular correlations. Chart 2.1 plots the intercorrelations from the two studies against each other. Generally speaking, the correlations from both studies correlate with each other. That is, symptoms which have a high correlation in one study tend to have a high correlation in the other; symptoms with low relationships in one study tend to have low relationships in the other. We find a value of +.62 for Yule's Q in the fourfold table created by dichotomizing each set at its median.

Such a confrontation gives us some perspective on the apparently contradictory conclusions of these two major studies. Since the two studies generally tend to agree when they ask the

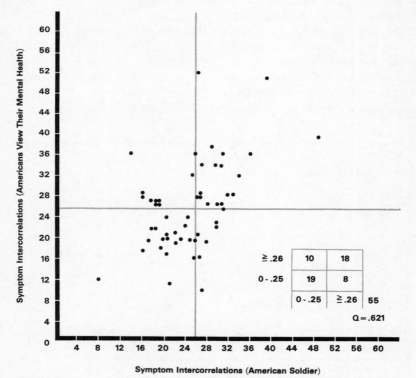

Chart 2.1 Graphic representation of data in Table 2.4

same questions and use identical statistical procedures, it would seem that differences in their content (items like "Lack of Uniqueness," "Parental Inadequacy," "Oversensitivity," "Identification with the War Effort," etc., which appear in one or the other but not in both studies) and the use of scales versus single items both play a large part in producing the apparent discrepancy. However, we must keep in mind that the agreement between the two studies is only relative, and even when identical procedures are used, identical results are not guaranteed. Table 2.5 singles out the intercorrelations for selected items with high loadings on the symptom factors extracted by Gurin, Veroff, and Feld. But let us note some discrepancies.

1. While "Shortness of Breath" and "Heart Beating Hard" have a very strong relationship (.52) in *Americans View Their Mental Health,* the relationship in *The American Soldier* (.26) is no higher than their correlations with other symptoms.
2. In *Americans View Their Mental Health,* "Health Problems" has a stronger relationship with the "Physical Anxiety" items than with the "Psychological Anxiety" items; the reverse is the case in *The American Soldier.*

Table 2.5 Intercorrelations for Items with High Symptom Factor Loadings (*Americans View Their Mental Health* and *The American Soldier*)*

Items	Physical Health (1)	Physical Anxiety (10) (6)	Psychological Anxiety (5) (2)	Immobilization (11)
Health problems (1)		36 26	25 24	11
Shortness of breath (10)	14	52	32 28	21
Heart beating hard (6)	19	26	34 24	20
Nervousness (5)	31	25 30	51	36
Sleep (2)	24	16 20	39	16
Hands clammy (11)	21	22 26	36 25	

*Shaded area from *The American Soldier,* white area from *Americans View Their Mental Health.* Numbering from item list in *The American Soldier.*

In short, while the relationships are generally similar, they are not so similar that we can find identical clusters or dimensions, even when the measures are presumably identical.

To summarize, part of the apparent discrepancy between the two studies comes from differences in content and statistical procedures. However, even when the data are comparable, the similarity between the studies is general, not specific. Just as a life table tells us that, generally speaking, seventy-year-olds are worse risks than twenty-year-olds (but it will not predict for specific seventy-year-olds or twenty-year-olds) these data tell us that, generally speaking, subjective measures of mental health are positively correlated, but they do not guarantee relatively high or relatively low agreement for specific pairs of items.

Unpublished data from an NORC survey shed some additional light on this problem. In 1958 NORC collected self-administered questionnaires from a national probability sample of 2,842 arts and science graduate students, representative of Master's and Ph.D. candidates in departments offering the Ph.D. in fields such as English, chemistry, history, psychology, etc. (see Davis, 1962). Since the aim of the study was to examine the financial problems of the students, a certain number of mental health questions were included to explore the possibility that financial problems contributed to students' maladjustment. Although certain data were reported in the volume *Stipends and Spouses* (Davis, 1962) no intercorrelation of the adjustment measures was undertaken. One was carried out for this report, however, on the following measures.

1. "Financial Worries": How much do you worry about your *immediate* financial situation?
2. "Spirits": In general, how would you say you feel most of the time—in good spirits or in low spirits?
3. "Good Time": In general, what sort of time do you have in graduate school—very good time, pretty good time, about fifty-fifty, pretty bad time, rotten time?
4. "Health": in general, how is your health at the present time?

   How often are you bothered by (the following)?
5. "Headaches."

6. "Insomnia."
7. "Periods of Feeling Blue."
8. "Periods When You Can't Force Yourself To Work."
9. "Worries about Schoolwork."
10. "Loss of Appetite."
11. "Confusion about Your Goals in Life."

Because questions 2 and 3 are taken from the "Personal Adjustment" scale in *The American Soldier*, and items 5, 6, 8, and 10 are like the items in symptom indices, it is interesting to see their intercorrelation in a young but highly educated recent sample (82 per cent male, 49 per cent married, 51 per cent twenty-seven or older, 100 per cent college graduate).

Table 2.6 gives the Q coefficients for the associations, grouped roughly as psychosomatic symptoms, general affective states (akin to "Happiness" in the Survey Research Center study and "Personal Adjustment" in *The American Soldier*), and content concerns (akin to "Soldier Role," etc., in *The American Soldier*, and "Social Inadequacy" in *Americans View Their Mental Health*). All but three of the coefficients ("Headaches" × "Goals," "Headaches" × "Financial Worries," "Insomnia" × "Financial Worries") are significant at the .01 level,[2] a pattern more like the data in *The American Soldier* than the findings of *Americans View Their Mental Health*. There are not enough common items to make a more specific comparison with the preceding studies, except that the average Q (.326) for the ten symptom intercorrelations in Table 2.4 is somewhat lower than Q values (.481) for the symptom item matrix from *The American Soldier*. (Q's tend to run higher than product-moment correlations on the same data.) Among the graduate students, then, psychosomatic symptoms, self-ratings of general affective states ("Good Spirits," "Blues"), and concerns about specific content areas ("Worries about Schoolwork," "Confusion about Goals in Life," "Good Time," and "Financial Worries") tend to have low but consistent positive associations.

A recent longitudinal study (Wilner *et al.*, 1962) of the effects

[2] Because the sample — although a true probability sample — is clustered, standard tables were entered with the value of .67 N rather than N.

Table 2.6 Q Coefficients of Association, Graduate Student Sample

Items	Symptoms					Affective States			Content Concerns		
	Health	Headaches	Insomnia	Can't Force Self To Work	Loss of Appetite	Spirits	Periods of Feeling Blue	Good Time	Worries about Schoolwork	Confusion about Goals in Life	Financial Worries
Health		.21	.38	.22	.46	.54	.33	.38	.29	.15	.16
Headaches			.43	.15	.32	.17	.28	.19	.27	.01	.12
Insomnia				.32	.47	.40	.48	.28	.42	.19	.12
Can't force self to work					.30	.43	.53	.32	.55	.40	.15
Loss of appetite							.50	.40	.60	.23	.19
Spirits							.77	.66	.43	.46	.32
Periods of feeling blue								.50	.47	.47	.24
Good time									.54	.37	.38
Worries about school-work										.41	.37
Confusion about goals in life											.14
Financial worries											

of public housing on physical and mental health provides further perspective on the problem by making available personal-interview data on a rather different sample (lower-class Negro women in Baltimore). We will discuss the study itself in the chapter on experiments, but for present purposes all we need to know is that families accepted for public housing were matched with families not yet accepted, and both were interviewed repeatedly from 1955 to 1958. Included in the schedule were a number of Guttman scales involving content similar to the scales we have reviewed. Professor Wilner was kind enough to make available unpublished product-moment correlations among the scales for 296 "experimental" women and 292 controls. The scales, and sample items, are as follows.

1. "Control of Temper": Is it often hard for you to control your temper? Are you the sort of person who almost never gets angry?
2. "Nervousness": Are you one of those persons who never gets nervous? Do you often feel that you are about to go to pieces?
3. "Mood": Do little things often make you feel blue? Are there times when you are so blue that you want to cry?
4. "Satisfaction with Personal State of Affairs": I'm really very happy about the way I've been getting along lately. Life is treating me pretty bad right now. Everything seems to go wrong with me nowadays.
5. "Optimism": It's hardly fair to bring a child into the world, the way things look for the future. If things seem to be going well for a while, there's usually some trouble right around the corner.
6. "Efficacy of Self-help": Things will get better only if you actually get out and do something to make them better. You can work hard and in the end you're back about where you started.
7. "Authoritarianism": What young people need most of all is strict discipline. A good leader doesn't have to be strict.

None of the scales is an exact duplicate of previously discussed measures, but comparisons are worth considering, since (*a*) "Nervousness" is one of the highest intercorrelating symptoms in *The American Soldier* and *Americans View Their Mental Health;* (*b*) "Mood" is somewhat akin to the "Personal Adjustment" scale in *The American Soldier,* "Happiness" in *Americans View Their Mental Health,* and "Spirits" in the graduate-student study (actually taken from *The American Soldier*'s "Personal Adjustment" scale; and (*c*) "Control of Temper" is analogous to "Oversensitivity" in *The American Soldier.* Table 2.7 gives the product-moment correlations from a middle wave of the interviewing. Coefficients for experimentals (N = 296) are given in the white portion of the table, controls (N = 292) in the shaded portion.

As in Table 2.2, these correlations can be arranged in a spectrum (or what Guttman calls a simplex structure) in which correlations between adjacent items are relatively high, but the values decline as one moves away toward either end of the list. (Formally, the criterion is that coefficients decline steadily as one moves away from the diagonal across rows or up and down columns.) Within the group of four measures that appear to be most similar to those we have been discussing, all the correlations except one (which is borderline) are significant. Optimism about the future, belief in the efficacy of self-help, and authoritarianism (not the "F" scale measure of "authoritarian personality") do not show consistent relationships with the more direct measures. Thus, the study confirms a trend which appears consistent in our review so far: Measures of symptoms and direct assessments of affective states tend to show low but consistent relationships, while more indirect and cognitive aspects ("Shortcomings in the Self," "Commitment to the War Effort," "Efficacy of Self-help," etc.) have very low or non-significant relationships. Even in the Survey Research Center data, symptoms and the direct assessment of happiness show mostly positive (although low) relationships.

The fifth study we will examine is the last involving self-ratings among a sample of adults and is based on four small samples of men, two (N = 87, 71) from university residences, and two (N = 52, 200) from military units. The report by Fiedler and his colleagues (Fiedler *et al.,* 1958) gives intercorrelations for four

Table 2.7 Intercorrelations from Baltimore Housing Study*

Scale Items	Analogous Scale Items				Unrelated Scale Items		
	Control of Temper	Nervous-ness	Mood	Personal Satisfaction	Optimism	Efficacy of Self-help	Authoritarianism
Control of temper		+.37	+.30	(+.18)	(+.17)	(+.03)	(−.11)
Nervousness	+.46		+.52	+.26	(+.16)	(+.18)	(−.00)
Mood	+.35	+.55		+.38	+.26	+.21	(+.02)
Personal satisfaction	+.32	+.45	+.38		+.45	+.40	(+.06)
Optimism	(+.16)	+.34	+.29	+.37		+.58	+.27
Efficacy of self-help	(+.14)	+.32	+.23	+.38	+.69		+.29
Authoritarianism	(+.02)	(+.18)	(+.05)	(+.10)	+.36	+.37	

*White area indicates coefficients for experimentals (N = 296); shaded area, for controls (N = 292). A personal communication from Professor Wilner indicates that all coefficients of .20 or greater are "significant." Coefficients of .19 or less are indicated by parentheses.

subjective measures and a number of behavioral and observer-rating items (health center visits, grade-point averages for students, disciplinary reports for soldiers, etc.) As the non-subjective measures show no consistent intercorrelations, Fiedler draws a negative conclusion: "Our data yield no evidence justifying the assumption that adjustment, in its present state of definition, should be considered a unitary trait in clinically unselected populations." While we are not yet ready to form a final opinion on Fiedler's conclusion, we can say that, if we consider only his subjective ratings, our familiar pattern of low positive intercorrelations appears. The subjective measures are the following.

1. Taylor Manifest Anxiety Scale: True-or-false answers to questions such as: "I am about as nervous as other people," "My sleep is often restless and disturbed," "Life is often a strain for me," "When embarrassed I often break out in a cold sweat, which is very annoying" (See Taylor, 1953).
2. "Self-esteem": Average favorableness of self-ratings on twenty-item semantic differential scales, e.g., "Friendly – Unfriendly," "Stable – Unstable."
3. "Self-satisfaction": Low discrepancies between semantic differential rating of self and ideal self.
4. General Army Adjustment Scale: Not described in the report but apparently somewhat like *The American Soldier*'s Personal Adjustment Scale; data available on only one of the two army samples.

Table 2.8 gives the product-moment correlations for the four samples.

Again we find the now familiar result — low positive intercorrelations. The significant associations between "Self-esteem" and the Taylor scale, however, are surprisingly high in view of the fact that *Americans View Their Mental Health* found no significant correlation between "Shortcomings in the Self" and "Felt Psychological Disturbance" or "Happiness," the former appearing to be much like "Self-esteem," and the latter, much like the content of the Taylor items. Thus, while Fiedler

Table 2.8 Intercorrelations of Self-ratings of College and Army Men in Fiedler (1958)

Subjective Measures	College Men				Army				
	Sample N 87		Sample N 71		Sample N 52		Sample N 200		
	Self-esteem	Taylor Scale	Self-esteem	Taylor Scale	Self-esteem	Taylor Scale	Self-esteem	Taylor Scale	Army Adjustment
Self-satisfaction	.60**	†	.55**	.34*	.36**	.37***	.44**	.30**	.15*
Self-esteem		†		.25		.43***		.34**	.16*
Taylor									.27*

* Significant at .05 level.
** Significant at .01 level.
† Data not collected.

may be justified in his pessimism regarding the correlation between self-ratings and performance indices such as grade-point
averages, health center visits, and visits to counseling centers
by students, within the self-rating data his results are consistent with the other studies we have reviewed.

Having reviewed (*a*) *The American Soldier,* (*b*) *Americans
View Their Mental Health,* (*c*) The NORC study of arts and
science graduate students, (*d*) data from Wilner's *Housing
Environment and Family Life,* and (*e*) Fiedler's studies of
soldiers and students, what conclusions can we draw? It is not
hard to state a general summary of the findings, but it is rather
difficult to assess their import. The "facts" appear to be the
following.

1. Measures of mental health based on subjective assessments
   of "psychosomatic" symptoms,[3] generalized affective states
   (happiness, spirits, blues, etc.), and feelings of hostility tend to
   show positive intercorrelations.
2. At the same time, the following conditions exist.
   a) The correlations are low, product-moment correlations
   from .25 to .35 being typical. Such relationships indicate
   that about 10 per cent of the variance in one measure can
   be accounted for by variance in the other.
   b) The structures and patterns of correlations are inconsistent
   from study to study.
   c) As one moves from directly perceived states of internal
   distress to more intellectualized aspects (e.g., "Shortcomings") or content issues (e.g., "Commitment to the
   War Effort," "Sociability"), the sizes of the correlations
   drop sharply.

Rather than supporting either a "unidimensional" òr "multi-
dimensional" interpretation, these results appear to provide arguments against both. The basic argument against a unidimen-

---

[3] It is important to stress that simply calling an item "psychosomatic" does
not make it psychosomatic. It may well be that headaches, insomnia, loss of
appetite, etc., have purely physical causes and that people experiencing physical
distress can hardly be expected to feel psychologically chipper.

sional interpretation (that mental health is a single entity and that all these items tap the same phenomenon in different degrees) is that the correlations are so low that, for practical purposes, the use of different items will lead to different results (examples of this will be seen in Chap. 3). However, the absence of uni-dimensionality does not mean that multiple dimensions of mental health can be discerned either, since no stable dimensions appear across studies, and some of the positive intercorrelations are surprising. For example, both *The American Soldier* and the Baltimore public housing study show a positive correlation between hostility and depressive states, which casts considerable doubt on the "obvious" distinction between internalization and externalization of hostility and on the "obviously" different dimensions of aggression and depression.

While the results are essentially ambiguous, and technical considerations intrude heavily (we might ask whether improved measurement would raise the correlations considerably or, conversely, whether the correlations which exist are an artifact of "response set"—a verbal habit of giving extreme answers to questions), we are inclined to suggest the following until more definitive results are obtained.

CONCLUSION 1

In the general population, individuals vary within a dimension of generalized subjective distress. Those people who are "high" in the dimension tend toward multiple complaints in the areas of (*a*) overall assessments of happiness, morale, spirits, blues, etc.; (*b*) feelings of hostility; (*c*) experiences of psychological tension—"nervousness," "tension," "high-strung"; (*d*) mild, multiple, and non-specific physical complaints—headaches, loss of appetite, insomnia, upset stomach, chronic tiredness, damp and clammy hands, mild irregularities of heart or respiration, trembling hands, "all sorts of pains and ailments in different parts of your body," etc.

RECOMMENDATION 1

Because of the multiple indicators of this dimension, and because of the low efficiency of measurement in these areas, research on generalized subjective distress should use multiple-item scales, rather than a single indicator, but analysis should be conducted on individual items as well as total scores.

Interrelations among experts' ratings. — Having considered similar responses from the same person, we can now shift to the question whether independent experts, evaluating detailed information on a given person, give similar ratings on mental health levels. Put this way, the question amounts to the statistical problem of the "reliability" of expert ratings.

Blum (1962) recently reviewed this literature, citing nearly twenty studies (many on clinical rather than normal populations), most of which draw rather pessimistic conclusions. Examples follow.

Pasamanick and his colleagues report significant differences between diagnostic classification proportions between [similar] wards within a hospital. . . .

Ash reports that three psychiatrists working in a clinic could agree on the major diagnostic category on only 45 per cent of the patients who were seen by each. . . .

Lilienfeld, reporting on field interviewers, found only a 55 per cent agreement between two interviewers.

Our impression is that such conclusions are unduly pessimistic, because they use perfection as their criterion. This point is important technically and substantively. From a technical point of view, most of these studies use as their measure either percentages of matches or significant differences in ratings. While significant differences in ratings are hardly desirable, their existence means merely that the raters do not agree perfectly. It does not mean that they disagree or even that they have a low level of agreement. Similarly, low percentages of matches are consistent with high levels of relative agreement. As a hypothetical example, if two psychiatrists rated cases on a one-hundred-point scale and were always one point apart in their ratings, they would show zero per cent agreement along with a fantastically high correlation.

From a substantive point of view, one should compare psychiatrists against the standard of available alternatives. We have just seen that different scales and questionnaire items set only a modestly competitive norm for reliability, and it can also be shown that other types of behavioral-science ratings show only moderate reliability. Heyns and Lippitt (1954), reviewing small-group observational techniques, show interobserver correlations for different observational systems with the following ranges: Bales Interaction Process Analysis, .75 to .95; Heyns Conference Research Problem-solving Category System, .64 to .97; Fouriezos, Hutt, and Guetzkow Self-oriented Need Observational System, .67 and .73; Carter's Observational Procedures, average of .68. Since these are all carefully defined systems for rating observable behavior — hardly the equivalent of abstract concepts such as mental health — psychiatric reliability would not have to be perfect to be well within standards of craftsmanship based on such systems.

An example from outside the laboratory underlines the point. In 1951–52, Sears, Maccoby, and Levin collected semistructured interviews from a sample of mothers of 379 kindergarten children in eight public schools in two suburbs of Boston (median age, 33.6; 22 per cent college graduates; 14 per cent less than high school; religious composition: "Protestant, Catholic, and Jewish faiths all strongly represented [*sic*]"). The children (the authors never report the number of mothers) comprised 79 per cent of the eligible children in the kindergartens (children of foreign-born parents, children from broken homes, twins, handicapped children, etc., were excluded). The eligibles themselves comprised 75 per cent of the children in the kindergartens (Sears *et al.*, 1957).

Ten carefully trained advanced graduate students independently rated the mothers on 188 scale dimensions, such as "Duration of Breast-feeding," "Amount of Pressure for Modesty," "Amount of Attention Child Wants," and "Mother's Evaluation of Father," on the basis of the interview transcripts. Rater reliabilities for 143 of the scales are reported in an appendix to the book. The average product-moment correlation (uncorrected for sample size) between pairs of raters was .703. Some of the reliabilities are very high (.948 for age at completion of weaning, .884 for mother's reported reaction to her pregnancy, .991 for the number of children in the family), but for the dimensions most akin to mental health ratings, reliabilities were considerably less. An example is the following.

32

Education for Positive Mental Health

Mother's self-esteem	.493
Mother's child-rearing anxiety	.485
Mother's attitude toward mother role	.517
Mother's evaluation of father	.636
Mother's dissatisfaction with current situation	.652

Thus, inter-rater correlations of .50 to .60 seem reasonable for careful ratings of psychological dimensions from interview protocols.

The only data[4] using correlation coefficients for ratings of mental health in normal populations come from a recent volume by Srole, Langner, Michael, Opler, and Rennie, *Mental Health in the Metropolis* (Srole *et al.,* 1962). The study will be considered in some detail later, but for now, all we need to report is that three psychiatrists on the staff of a research project rated the overall mental health of 228 respondents sampled from New York City, basing their ratings on lengthy personal-interview questionnaires. The intercorrelations, in terms of product-moment coefficients, are given in Table 2.9 (Srole *et al.,* 1962, p. 400).

The results are hardly definitive: the fact that the three psychiatrists were long-term collaborators on a research project probably enhances their agreement; the three are not representative of psychiatrists or clinical psychologists; we are not told how the 228 cases were selected; we are not told what steps were

[4]This statement and all subsequent similar statements should be interpreted to mean that there is only one such study of adequate technical quality that we found during our limited search of the literature in English.

Table 2.9 Intercorrelations of Psychiatrists' Ratings (N = 228)

Psychiatrist	Psychiatrist		
	Rennie	Michael	Kirkpatrick
Rennie		.77	.61
Michael			.68
Kirkpatrick			

taken to insure that the ratings were independent; and so on. At the same time, these correlations compare favorably with the correlations among subjective measures and are about the same as those reviewed above for small-group observational schemes.

Obviously, the degree of agreement can be improved, and we need further studies of this kind, but our impression is that the "unreliability of psychiatric ratings" has been oversold and has become an unrealistic obstacle to research in mental health (partly because it serves as a rationalization for the continuing battles between behavioral scientists and psychiatrists, whose collaborations have often been stormy indeed).

Furthermore, we believe that the problem is not terribly important from the viewpoint of research. From the viewpoint of practice, the fact that there is low reliability among practitioners raises a large number of important policy problems, but in terms of research, it is well known that rater reliability can be increased by (*a*) breaking down the rating task into specific, simple parts; (*b*) improving the clarity of the definitions; (*c*) improving the training of raters; and (*d*) providing sufficient and appropriate information for ratings. Seen in this way, the low reliability of psychiatric ratings appears to stem from characteristics peculiar to psychiatrists but from the fact that they have been asked to rate abstract, fuzzy dimensions from fuzzy data. Thus, our prediction is that if further studies are conducted (or a better review of the literature discloses a number of such studies), more of the disparity will come from inaccuracies in the dimensions to be rated and the information provided than from variation among psychiatrists. At one extreme, one would expect a high agreement on "the degree to which the person is prevented from carrying on daily activities," as assessed from lengthy, structured personal-interview schedules, and at the other extreme, a low agreement on "capacity to give and receive love" on the basis of thirty-minute informal interviews.

At the same time, it would improve one's ability to assess research results if there were a standardized rating system, containing known reliabilities, which would be used routinely in mental health research, much as symptom check-lists and the Taylor Manifest Anxiety Scale are becoming.

CONCLUSION 2

The slim evidence available on the reliability of psychiatric ratings of the mental health of normal populations is that, while reliability is low, it is no worse than other measurement and rating techniques which are accepted without question.

RECOMMENDATION 2

Technical research should be conducted, using available interview protocols on representative populations and a fairly large number of psychiatrists and clinical psychologists, to develop reliable[5] rating procedures for assessing mental health, setting as a goal the attainment of product-moment correlations of .90 or higher between independent, "blind" raters after training of one day's duration or less.

RECOMMENDATION 3

Research using expert raters should use the pooled ratings of two or more raters, each of whom is required to give independent assessments of the same materials on a common rating scale or category system.

The Problem of Degree

Although closely associated with the problem of dimensionality, the problem of degree of mental health is slightly different. Even if one accepts the conclusion that there is a general phenomenon which can be called "mental health," two important questions are left open. First, how healthy is the American population? Second, is mental illness the extreme end of the continuum?

This section will be relatively brief, because we have been unable to unearth research which provides anything like an answer to either of these problems. We have considered the measurement of mental health in some detail without considering the obvious question: "How healthy is the general population?" In spite of the fact that certain studies have come up with numbers (*Mental Health in the Metropolis*, for example, suggests the well-publicized figure of 23.4 per cent "impaired" and reviews several similar studies [Srole *et al.*, 1962, pp. 138–45]), it is our opinion that existing techniques of measurement cannot yield meaningful estimates of overall levels of mental health. The

[5] Reliability, of course, is different issue from "validity." This does not, however, make it an unimportant issue.

reason is technical but simple: all existing measures provide orderings or rankings of subjects, not assessments of levels. The question has nothing to do with reliability and validity, but rather with the logic of measurement. The existing measures of mental health are like beauty contests, in which judges may be able to order the contests quite reliably, and their order may show a high correlation with some "true" measure of beauty, but at the same time the results cannot tell us how many girls in the contest are beautiful. The judges could be working with a populaton of raving beauties or unattractive girls; the ranking does not betray this.

For purposes of presentation or statistical analysis, it is often useful to attach numbers to these scales or divide them into "high," "medium," and "low," but without an outside criterion, such operations have meaning only within the sample. Thus, except in the trivial sense (e.g., "half the population is below average in mental health"; "—— per cent of the population falls below a point we have arbitrarily chosen to call mentally healthy," etc.), these measures are only useful for internal comparisons. For example, it is meaningful to conclude that "people in this community are more likely to fall below the arbitrary cutting point than people in that community." But such measures have no intrinsic meaning.

CONCLUSION 3
Measures of mental health, using existing techniques, are meaningful only for assessing relative differences among population groups, not absolute levels.

We must draw a similar negative conclusion in response to the important question whether extremely bad mental health is to be equated with mental illness. A keystone in the assumptions of mental health education is the idea that below a certain point on measures of mental health one would chiefly find either people in mental hospitals or non-hospitalized persons who would be diagnosed as mentally ill, but there is no evidence to substantiate it. It is not our intent to review here the entire literature on mental illness, but we feel that a detailed review would support the following generalizations.

1. The etiology of the so-called functional psychoses is unknown today.
2. Hospitalization or outpatient treatment for mental illness is so heavily influenced by extraclinical factors (the availability of treatment facilities, attitudes toward psychotherapy, families' tolerance of and facilities for maintaining a malfunctioning member in the home, court and police definitions of deviance, etc.) that it does not provide an appropriate research measure of mental illness.
3. There has been no study of a normal population which showed that persons with unfavorable scores on measures of generalized subjective distress are more likely to develop psychoses or neuroses.

We quickly grant that there is no evidence against the idea either, but the mental health educator's assumption that attempts to improve the mental health of "normals" help to prevent severe mental illness is a matter of faith, not a conclusion based on research evidence. This does not mean that amelioration of worries, unhappiness, psychosomatic symptoms, hostilities, etc., is not a justifiable end in itself, but such efforts cannot be justified today in terms of demonstrable efficacy of "prevention."

CONCLUSION 4
There is no research evidence for or against the assumption that mental illness is the extreme form of the phenomenon we have called generalized subjective distress.

RECOMMENDATION 4
High priority should be given to longitudinal studies of the relationship between generalized subjective distress and mental illness. In particular, because of the lengthy time intervals, special priority should be given to studies in which large samples of people whose mental health was assessed previously are followed up to determine, at the least, hospitalization or treatment, but preferably current mental illness and adjustment.

ACCEPTANCE OF PRINCIPLES OF ADJUSTMENT
Having reviewed the status of research states of adult mental health, let us turn to studies dealing with the principles of mental

hygiene which are assumed to affect mental health and whose dissemination plays such a large role in mental health education programs. Because of the assumed importance of child-rearing, we shall treat principles of adult adjustment first and then separately consider principles of child development.

What the General Population and Experts Believe

We found three published studies presenting data on cross-sections of the general population and their beliefs about principles of adult adjustment and prevention of mental illness (Ramsey and Seipp, 1948; Woodward, 1951; Nunnally, 1961). Two of them are fairly brief, but the third is a major study with a wealth of important detailed information. We will begin with the research reported by Nunnally (1961) in his *Popular Conceptions of Mental Health*. Nunnally proceeded as follows.

1. A pool of over 3,000 items was collected from mental hygiene books, professional publications, and mental health pamphlets.
2. The pool was reduced to 240 items by removal of apparent duplicates, and items were reworded so that a random half were reversed in meaning (to offset any tendency for some subjects to give consistent "yes" or "no" answers).
3. The 240-item questionnaire was administered to a non-probability sample of 349 persons living in the vicinity of Champaign-Urbana, Illinois (54 per cent male; 72 per cent Protestant; 23 per cent less than high school; 38 per cent college graduate; 70 per cent married; 54 per cent forty or older, with an age range from fifteen to over ninety.[6]

Respondents were asked to check each item using a seven-point scale with extremes labeled "Disagree" and "Agree." An example is the following.

	Disagree						Agree
X-rays of the head will tell whether a person is likely to develop insanity.	1	2	3	4	5	6	7

[6] No date reported for the administration of the questionnaire, but presumably it was in 1955 or 1956.

Appendix I of the book gives the distributions of the 349 subjects for each of the 240 items. Because a large number of the items deal with characteristics of mental patients and mental hospitals (e.g., "The insane have facial expressions like those of normals"; "Few of the people in mental hospitals require special diets"), which are not at the core of our concern, we shall consider a selected group of items dealing with adjustment problems of normal adults and with ideas about the causes and prevention of mental illness.

In a later study reported in the book, Nunnally submitted some of these items to a national probability sample of mental health experts. Responses are reported for 176 experts, distributed as follows: 86 out of a sample of 150 psychologists selected from the files of the American Psychological Association, 75 of whom were randomly selected from diplomates in clinical psychology and 75 from diplomates in counseling and guidance; 90 out of the 150 psychiatrists who were members of the Group for Advancement of Psychiatry. Experts were asked to rate the generalization behind each item in terms of whether its position should be repudiated or supported in public information programs. The scale was designed in the manner below.

Repudiate			Omit			Support
1	2	3	4	5	6	7

We took the raw numbers in the general-population data and compared the total cases checking 1 or 2 with the total cases checking 6 and 7, then divided the larger of these by the total. Below is a more graphic demonstration. The figure of 48 per cent

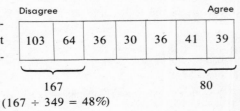

Showing a great deal of affection to a child can prevent him from developing independence.

Disagree						Agree
103	64	36	30	36	41	39

167

80

$(167 \div 349 = 48\%)$

means that 48 per cent of the total disagreed with the statement and that disagreement was more common than agreement. The resulting index combines the position of the public with its extent of homogeneity, low figures suggesting low homogeneity. Thus a figure of 33 per cent "Agree" means that even though agreement was more common than disagreement, only one-third of the sample took the modal position. A similar procedure was followed when the experts rated the same item. The accompanying tabulation gives the results on adjustment problems of normal

Statement on Questionnaire	Champaign Sample		Experts' Judgments	
	Modal Response	Per Cent	Position	Per Cent
Short men are less likely to have feelings of inferiority than men of average height	Disagree	63		
A person can avoid worry by keeping busy	Agree	61	Repudiate	27
An emotionally upset person will become calmer if he talks about his problems	Agree	60		
Ulcers are most frequently found in un-aggressive-acting people	Disagree	60		
It is harmful to a person's mental health to let others dominate him	Agree	58		
Jealousy is a sign of feelings of inferiority	Agree	58		
We dislike people who show the qualities that we dislike in ourselves	Agree	55		
The best way to get over a fear of high places is to gradually get used to them	Agree	54		
A job promotion is usually helpful in curing a person's inferiority complex	Agree	54		
Shyness is not inherited	Agree	50		
Inferiority complexes often occur in people with high abilities	Agree	50		
Aggressive people are usually more sure of themselves	Agree	49		
People of average intelligence are usually more popular than people of high intelligence	Agree	48		
People who have been reared in prosperous environments enjoy adult life more than those who have been reared in poor circumstances	Disagree	47		
Anger is never simply forgotten—it comes out in one way or another	Agree	46		
Criminals have more nervous breakdowns than other people	Disagree	46		
It is injurious to a person's mental health to think a great deal about any one problem	Agree	45		

(Continued)

Continued

Statement on Questionnaire	Champaign Sample		Experts' Judgments	
	Modal Response	Per Cent	Position	Per Cent
Emotionally unstable people act nervous only when others are around	Disagree	44		
"In-law" trouble is the largest cause of divorce	Disagree	43		
People remember unpleasant events longer than pleasant ones	Agree	40		
People who go from doctor to doctor with many complaints know that there is nothing really wrong with them	Disagree	38	Repudiate	72
If you try acting as though you like someone, you will learn to like him eventually	Agree	37		
People with college educations have less trouble solving their emotional problems	Disagree	36		
Men worry more than women	Disagree	35	Repudiate	23
People who are in good physical condition seldom have emotional upsets	Agree	35		
Emotionally upset persons are seldom found in important positions in business	Agree	34	Support	37
A person can rid himself of unpleasant memories if he tries hard enough to forget them	Agree	34	Repudiate	59
It would improve anyone's mental health to spend a certain amount of time each day thinking over his emotional problems	Disagree	31		
Emotionally healthy people do not try to hold back their emotions	Agree	30	Support	65
If a person concentrates on happy memories, he will not be bothered by unpleasant things in the present	Agree	29	Repudiate	47
Boys are more likely to develop a "nervous disposition" if they have no father, rather than no mother	Disagree	29		

adults, ranked in order of percentage size, with the experts' ratings given in some instances.

Because idiosyncracies of question-wording make large differences in the percentages of agreement on attitude items, one should exercise caution in drawing inferences, particularly since Nunnally did not have a probability sample. However, the results for these thirty-one items suggest the following ideas, most of which are noted by Nunnally in his general conclusions.

1. The public is far from unanimous on these questions: no item received two-thirds endorsement or rejection, and nineteen

out of the thirty received less than 50 per cent in the modal category.

2. Most of the items receiving high endorsement are bits and pieces of popularized psychology (ulcers and aggressiveness, "inferiority complexes") and platitudes ("An emotionally upset persons will become calmer if he talks about his problems"), not folk beliefs or principles flatly rejected by the experts.

3. Public beliefs are contradictory (e.g., you should not hold back your emotions, but if you concentrate on happy memories you will not be bothered by unpleasant things).

4. The closest to a discrepancy between experts and the general public seems to be in the area of "denial." The public believes that keeping busy, trying to forget, and concentrating on happy memories helps solve distress, but the experts oppose these ideas.

Turning now to beliefs about the etiology of mental illness and "nervous breakdowns" among adults, we get results indicated in the tabulation below. Again, considering the tentative inferences that can be drawn from such data, we suggest the ideas that follow.

Statement on Questionnaire	Champaign Sample		Experts' Judgments	
	Modal Response	Per Cent	Position	Per Cent
A person's mental illness may come from having a spell cast on him by a fortune teller	Disagree	86		
Insanity is not brought on as a punishment for sins	Agree	83		
People who live in the country are more likely to become insane than people who live in large cities	Disagree	75		
Many nervous breakdowns could be prevented if people changed to jobs that fit them better	Agree	74		
Nervous breakdowns seldom occur among people in high income groups	Disagree	74		
Worry over health brings on many emotional problems	Agree	72		

Continued

Statement on Questionnaire	Champaign Sample		Experts' Judgments	
	Modal Response	Per Cent	Position	Per Cent
People who belong to clubs and social organizations are more likely to develop mental illness than those who do not	Disagree	70		
People who do a variety of things in their work are more likely to have a nervous breakdown than those who do routine jobs	Disagree	69		
One severe fright does not make a person "nervous" for the rest of his life	Agree	65		
Financial worries are seldom the cause of nervous breakdowns	Disagree	60		
Women who have no children are less likely to develop emotional disorders	Disagree	59		
If a person's mind is going to "crack," nothing can prevent it	Disagree	58		
"Nervousness" is not a sign of oncoming insanity	Agree	56		
Most people can recognize the type of person who is likely to have a nervous breakdown	Disagree	54	Repudiate	77
A confession of sins will not prevent insanity	Agree	53		
If a person has more than the average amount of sexual relations, it can drive him insane	Disagree	52		
Mental disorders are more widespread than they were twenty years ago	Agree	51		
Some people are born with the kind of nervous system that makes it easy for them to become emotionally disturbed	Agree	50		
Insanity comes about gradually	Agree	50		
A nervous breakdown will grow into insanity if help is not given	Agree	47		
People who have little sexual desire are less likely to have a "nervous breakdown" than are other people	Disagree	45	Repudiate	49
If a person says he is "going crazy," there is little chance that he will do so	Agree	46		
Most of the people who have had nervous breakdowns have had more real problems than normal people	Disagree	45		
Normal men do not become mental cases in the stress of battle	Disagree	43		
People who attend church regularly are as likely to end up in a mental hospital as those who do not	Disagree	42		
More men than women have nervous breakdowns	Disagree	37	Repudiate	29
Normal people cannot suddenly become insane	Disagree	35		
Highly educated people are more likely to "lose their minds" than other people	Disagree	35		

Continued

Statement on Questionnaire	Champaign Sample		Experts' Judgments	
	Modal Response	Per Cent	Position	Per Cent
Nervous breakdowns usually come after a person has had some personal tragedy	Agree	35		
A nervous breakdown can often be avoided by moving to a different city	Disagree	33	Repudiate	45
People who are likely to have a nervous breakdown pay little attention to their personal appearance	Disagree	31	Repudiate	45
People who appear nervous and fidgety are the most likely to have a nervous breakdown	Disagree	25		
Financial trouble is the most frequent cause of nervous breakdowns	Disagree	24		
Books on "peace of mind" prevent many people from developing nervous breakdowns	Agree	23	Repudiate	21

1. The general public strongly rejects folklore on mental illness (spells, punishments for sin), and although very few of the items were given to the experts, there is general agreement between public and experts on the four comparable questions.
2. The general public accepts the "current environment" hypothesis of mental health education, giving fairly high assent to the suggestion that mental illness can stem from job problems, health difficulties, and financial problems.
3. The general public appears confused on the problem of whether some people are "prone" to mental illness, independent of environmental stress; items dealing with predisposition showed lower percentages, and hence less consensus.

At this point it may be well to review briefly the two other studies which bear on public beliefs about the etiology of mental illness. Woodward (1951), reporting on an area probability sample of 3,971 Louisville, Kentucky, adults interviewed in 1950, says that 72 per cent of the sample answered "false" to the statement, "Most mental illness is inherited." However, an indirect measure yielded some doubts that the population really associates behavioral stresses with mental illness. Respondents were read the following:

Mr. G., a fifty-two-year-old machinist . . . had always been a hard worker who had worried a lot about making both ends meet for his large family. One day his job at the plant was given to someone else and he was told by his employer that he was no longer needed. After this happened, he became very depressed, accused himself of being a complete failure and worthless to his family. He refused to look for another job or to take an interest in anything and finally tried to commit suicide.

Remembering that clear majorities of the Nunnally sample endorsed various versions of the idea that job problems can lead to mental breakdowns, it is interesting to see what the Louisville sample recommended from a forced-choice list of actions, shown in Table 2.10. Considering that Woodward reports 81 per cent of the Louisville sample agreed that "It's always worthwhile to get a psychiatrist's help when someone begins to act queerly or get strange ideas," and assuming that the populations of Louisville and Champaign are comparable, the distinct suggestion is that the general population fails to translate its abstract accep-

Table 2.10 Louisville Study of Public Beliefs about Mental Illness

Action Presumably Indicating Situation Was:	Per Cent
Not defined as mental illness:	
His family and friends should give him a good pep talk and urge him to look for another job	33
He should have a good long rest away from his family responsibilities and worries	15
He should be given plenty of time to recover from shock of losing his job and then he'll be all right again	14
None of them, don't know	9
Total	71
Defined as mental illness:	
He should be sent to a psychiatrist for consultation and treatment	11
He should be sent to a mental hospital for asylum until he is better	2
Total	13
Indeterminate:	
He should go to his family doctor to find out if there is a physical illness that is causing him to feel bad	16
Grand total	100
N	3,971

tance of mental health principles into appropriate responses in concrete situations.

The final study by Ramsey and Seipp (1948) is based on a quota sample of 345 respondents in Trenton, New Jersey, interviewed during the late 1940's. Overall results on relevant items are shown in Table 2.11. Since the "living conditions" question is hopelessly ambiguous, all we can conclude is that this study is in agreement with the other two in its very low acceptance of folklore and its lack of consensus on predisposing factors, in this example, heredity.

The Nunnally data are so rich and reported in such full detail that it is worthwhile to return to that study to consider two additional problems—the degree of structuring of lay opinions and the degree of consensus among the experts. In order to examine

Table 2.11   Results of Trenton, New Jersey, Study

Statement and Responses	Per Cent
Do you or do you not think that insanity is inherited?	
Yes, unqualified	22
Qualified	40
No, unqualified	32
Don't know	6
Total	100
N	345
Some people believe that poor living conditions are a cause of insanity. Others disagree. What is your opinion?	
Agree	27
Qualified agreement	19
Disagree	52
Don't know	2
Total	100
N	280
Do you believe that insanity is God's punishment for some sin or wrongdoing?	
Yes	14
Yes, qualified	7
No	74
Don't know	5
Total	100
N	344

the pattern of interrelations among the items, Nunnally subjected 180 of the 240 items to factor analysis, excluding sixty items that varied only slightly. Ten factors were extracted and are described in the book. More important, however, are Nunnally's (1961) general conclusions, given below.

> Public Information is not highly structured. . . . Correlations among the items were generally low. The average correlation, disregarding sign, was about .25. The factors which were derived were not statistically strong. Few of the loadings were above .40 and the first ten centroid factors explained less than 25 per cent of the total item variance. . . . People are unsure of the correctness of their information and will change their opinions readily. . . . People often agree with inconsistent statements or fail to agree with apparently consistent statements.

Nunnally's own conclusions will serve to summarize our review of materials on the beliefs of the general public.

CONCLUSION 5
1. The average man rejects the superstitions and obvious misconceptions about mental health (Nunnally, 1961).
2. The public is *uninformed*, in the sense that the average man has little information, correct or incorrect, about many of the problems (Nunnally, 1961, p. 232).
3. What information he has exists largely as an abstract system (Nunnally, 1961, p. 28), which is ignored, rather than rejected in practical life situations.

To which we add the following.

4. In the abstract, the general population accepts the idea that environmental stress leads to mental illness, but it has few firm opinions on predisposing factors.

After analyzing similar data on the questions submitted for expert evaluation, Nunnally (1961, p. 36) concluded, "Experts are in reasonable agreement about some aspects of a public information program." Even though the conclusion is carefully hedged, our evaluation of the same figures is less optimistic. To begin with, Nunnally bases his conclusion on the fact that the item-variances of the experts seem about one-half those for the general public; thus experts show less disparity. However, this demonstrates only *relative* agreement. When absolute levels of agreement are considered, and gross fallacies are excluded (e.g., 88 per cent of the experts agreed that mental health programs should repudiate the idea that "most people who 'go crazy' try to kill themselves") agreement on personal-adjustment techniques and prevention of mental illness is far from clear. The experts' responses, percentaged as above, are shown in the accompanying tabulation.

Of the seventeen items, only three drew two-thirds endorsement from the experts, and these tend to be denials that principles exist: trying hard to control emotions is not helpful; people with

Statement and Modal Response	Per Cent in Modal Category
Adjustment problems:	
People who go from doctor to doctor with many complaints know that there is nothing really wrong with them (Repudiate)	72
Mental health is largely a matter of trying hard to control the emotions (Repudiate)	65
A person cannot rid himself of unpleasant memories by trying hard to forget them (Support)	59
If a person concentrates on happy memories, he will not be bothered by unpleasant things in the past (Repudiate)	47
Emotionally upset persons are often found in important positions in business (Support)	37
Women have no more emotional problems than men do (Support)	30
A person can avoid worry by keeping busy (Repudiate)	27
Men worry more than women (Repudiate)	25
Etiology:	
Most people can recognize the type of person who is likely to have a nervous breakdown (Repudiate)	77
Almost any disease that attacks the nervous system is likely to bring on insanity (Repudiate)	67
People who have little sexual desire are less likely to have a "nervous breakdown" than are other people (Repudiate)	49
People who are likely to have a nervous breakdown pay little attention to their personal appearance (Repudiate)	45
Physical rest will not prevent a mental disorder (Support)	37
Physical exhaustion does not lead to a nervous breakdown (Support)	35
Adult problems are less important in causing emotional disorders than the individual's childhood experiences (Repudiate)	31
More women than men have nervous breakdowns (Repudiate)	29
Books on "peace of mind" prevent many people from developing nervous breakdowns (Repudiate)	21

a potential for mental illness cannot be recognized; diseases of the nervous system do not always bring on insanity. At the opposite extreme, on the crucial principle of predisposition versus stress, there is only a 31 per cent choice of the modal position. More important, perhaps, is the negative tone of the entire set. The experts, naturally, could react only to the items that Nunnally presented, but unless Nunnally deliberately withheld positive, practical ideas, it is difficult to find on his list a single positive suggestion for mental health improvement which the experts endorse. The experts are against peace-of-mind books, physical rest, keeping busy, concentrating on happy memories, neurological explanations, and attempting to control the emotions, but it is hard to find anything they are "for."

The experts are not withholding precious secrets from the laity, for the obvious reason that there is no set of practical techniques for mental hygiene, backed by research and endorsed by a majority of the experts. The point is important (and is the reason why this research was commissioned), but important points are often overlooked. The mental hygienist is in a position very different from that of the political propagandist, the money-raiser, the classroom teacher, or the merchandiser, simply because, although he feels it is tremendously important to inform the public, the only information he has is a rejection of extreme beliefs which the public does not hold anyway.

CONCLUSION 6
While the experts are in fair agreement on fallacies of mental health, they have no set of practical, positive actions to recommend to the general population regarding personal adjustment and the prevention of mental illness.

Correlates of Acceptance
We can complete our review of acceptance of principles of adult mental health by considering briefly what is known about population differences in acceptance of these principles. Again, we shall rely heavily on Nunnally's book.

On the basis of his factor analysis, Nunnally prepared a new questionnaire, limited to fifty items showing high loading on the factors. (It was this questionnaire which was given to the experts, which explains why so few of the preceding items were rated by both experts and the Champaign sample.) The new schedule was administered to "an area sampling" *(sic)* of 201 respondents in Knoxville, Tennessee, and to an undefined sample of 150 subjects in Eugene, Oregon, "consisting mostly of couples with young children." Added to the original Champaign sample, they give a total of 700 respondents answering the items in the revised questionnaire. In *Popular Conceptions of Mental Health* (Nunnally, 1961), zero-order correlations of "Education," "Income," "Age," and "Sex" with factor scores for the ten dimensions are reported for this pooled sample of 700 subjects. The results are submitted in Table 2.12.

Limiting our attention to the four factors most closely associated with mental health principles as defined here, we see that the correlations, though small, are as one would expect. The population groups who would be expected to be well informed (the highly educated, the well-to-do, and the young) reject the idea that will power or avoidance of morbid thoughts are effective mental hygiene principles. High education and income are associated with a rejection of organic causes, while youth (but not education) is associated with the personality-dynamics theory of mental illness.

Table 2.12 Correlations between Beliefs about Mental Health and Demographic Variables Significant at the .01 Level

Factor	Education	Income	Age	Sex (Female)
II. Will power†	−.35	−.28	+.18	*
IV. Avoidance of morbid thoughts‡	−.24	−.17	+.38	+.10
VII. External Environment v. personality dynamics§	*	*	+.16	+.10
X. Organic causes#	−.21	−.16	*	−.11

* Not significant at the .01 level.

† Will power is the basis of personal adjustment. Persons who remain mentally ill do not "try" to get better. Most of the people who seek treatment do not need it.

‡ Preoccupation with pleasant thoughts is the basis of mental health. Mental disturbances can be avoided by keeping busy, reading books on "peace of mind," and not discussing troublesome topics.

§ Mental troubles are caused by physical exhaustion or financial and social problems. A cure can be effected by a vacation or change of scenery. The opposite view is that the individual's state of well-being is dependent on his personal history, especially his childhood.

Mental disorder is brought on by organic factors such as poor diet and diseases of the nervous system.

It is always difficult to interpret age differences, since they may follow from the experience of aging or the differential experience of different historical generations, but we believe these data support the idea that over the years the general public (whether through formal education, mass media, or mental health education programs) is being pulled toward the positions endorsed by mental health experts. The point is so obvious that it hardly needs complete documentation, but it does provide indirect evidence for the important idea that public opinion has and can be modified. Among the other studies pointing in this direction are the following.

1. Myers (1955) compared physicians under and over fifty in a sample of New Jersey doctors not specializing in psychiatry or neurology and concluded:

   Young physicians indicated a greater interest in psychiatry, an apparently greater awareness of mental health problems, and a greater amount of factual information about psychiatric facilities in the state.

2. Hunter (1957, p. 38) in reporting on a 1955 study of New Orleans teachers, reviewed a number of additional studies, all of which show over the years an increasing convergence of teachers' and mental health experts' ratings of the seriousness of specific children's behavior problems since Wickman's (1928) study.

3. As part of his series of studies, Nunnally (1961, p. 100) polled a representative sample of members of the American Academy of General Practice and concluded:

   It is clear that younger doctors are more sensitive to symptoms of mental illness in their patients, are more likely to treat such patients themselves, see these problems in terms of personality development, rather than as matters of will power, and put less faith in tranquilizing drugs.

4. Ramsey and Seipp (1948) show that higher education and youth are associated with rejection of the idea that insanity is hereditary, God's punishment, or due to "poor living conditions."

5. Woodward (1951), in his Louisville study, states:

> The age breakdowns on nearly all of the questions show a clear-cut differential between the old and the young, with the latter uniformly the more "humanitarian." The young are also nearly always more "scientific" in viewpoint in the sense that they more often favor calling in professional help. . . . The same contrasts appear in the breakdowns by education.

Since the young are much better educated in the general population, and none of the general population studies holds education constant in its age comparisons, the conclusions of such studies are not firm. Nevertheless, the age differences among physicians and teachers in effect hold constant the level of education and support the idea of historical change, particularly since the Hunter (1957) study reviews research over a number of years.

CONCLUSION 7
The general effect of information flow in the United States is to increase the agreement between the population and mental health experts, and those persons most exposed to information show the greatest agreement.

PRINCIPLES OF CHILD DEVELOPMENT

It is not our aim to review here the entire literature on child development and personality, an academic area which is in itself a specialized discipline. Furthermore, Brim's (1959) book, *Education for Child Rearing,* attempts such a review from the viewpoint of programs for parent education. Rather we shall limit our attention to two problems: (*a*) what the general population and the experts believe, and (*b*) what are the correlates of acceptance.

What the General Public and the Experts Believe

While much study has been devoted to what parents do, the question of what parents believe has received little attention, undoubtedly because of the feeling that in child-rearing "actions speak louder than words." We return once more to Nunnally's Champaign sample for our only information. Repeating our percentaging procedure for the general population and the experts,

Statement on Questionnaire	Champaign Sample		Experts' Judgments	
	Modal Response	Per Cent	Position	Per Cent
Children become tense when their parents are upset	Agree	89		
Telling a child that you don't love him is usually more disturbing to him than giving him a spanking	Agree	85		
Affection is less important to the child's development than financial security	Disagree	85		
Noisy children are more likely to become emotionally disordered adults than quiet ones	Disagree	67		
Children can have nervous break-downs	Agree	65		
Offering rewards is a poor way to cure a child of thumb-sucking	Agree	61		
A child cannot inherit fears directly from his mother	Agree	60		
A boy inherits his emotional dis-position from his mother	Disagree	57		
Fathers have more influence than mothers on the emotional devel-opment of their children	Disagree	56		
Disappointments do not affect chil-dren as much as they do adults	Disagree	55	Repudiate	33
Parents can build self-confidence in a child by complimenting him a great deal	Agree	54		
A child will not develop a liking for people unless he is taught	Disagree	53		
If a mother is nervous and upset when pregnant, it may make the child emotionally unstable	Disagree	51		
The adult who needs a great deal of affection is likely to have had lit-tle affection in childhood	Agree	51	Support	34
If a child is jealous of a younger brother, it is best not to let him show it in any way	Disagree	48	Repudiate	83
Showing a great deal of affection to a child can prevent him from de-veloping independence	Disagree	48		
People who have been reared in prosperous environments enjoy adult life more than those who have been reared in poor circum-stances	Disagree	47		
Children usually forget about frightening experiences in a short time	Disagree	45	Repudiate	44

Continued

Statement on Questionnaire	Champaign Sample		Experts' Judgments	
	Modal Response	Per Cent	Position	Per Cent
Children who move from city to city are more likely to develop an emotional disorder than those who grow up in one neighborhood	Agree	42		
There is no way of telling from a child's behavior whether or not he will become insane in later life	Agree	42		
Parents encourage mental disorder if they severely threaten their children	Agree	41		
Girls are more likely to develop a mental disorder if they have no father rather than no mother	Disagree	40		
An emotional shock in childhood is seldom responsible for adult mental disorder	Agree	38		
Good emotional habits can be taught to children in school as easily as spelling can	Agree	37	Repudiate	42
If a child is "bossed" around a great deal, he is likely to boss everyone else around when he grows up	Agree	35		
Mental disorders have their beginnings in childhood	Agree	31		
Boys are more likely to develop a "nervous disposition" if they have no father rather than no mother	Disagree	29		
An only child is more likely to grow into a neurotic adult	Agree	28		
Boys and girls who start dating at an early age are less likely to develop emotional disorders	Disagree	28		
If a girl has sexual relations before she is mature, it can lead to a mental disorder	Agree	23		

the results shown in the accompanying tabulation are found for items on child development. While the average percentage for these items is little different from the averages for the items on adult adjustment and prevention of mental illness, we note three items for which there is unusual assent—the only items reviewed here with more than 80 per cent in the modal category. Interestingly, all three deal with emotional relationships: the idea that children are affected negatively by parents' emotional upsets, the idea that affection is more important than financial security, and the idea that the withdrawal of love is disturbing to a child.

Three items in a non-probability sample in Champaign, Illinois, hardly constitute firm documentation (actually there is a fourth item — 48 per cent *reject* the idea that showing a great deal of affection prevents the development of independence), but, in contrast to the hodgepodge of essentially negative propositions reviewed in consideration of adult mental health, these results suggest that contemporary Americans have a fairly specific theory of child-rearing. We can put it as follows.

1. A child's emotional development is relatively unaffected by the following factors.
   a) Heredity: A child cannot inherit fears directly.
   b) Material environment: People who have been reared in prosperous environments do not enjoy adult life more than those who have been reared in poor circumstances.
   c) Manipulation of rewards: Offering rewards is a poor way to cure a child of thumb-sucking.
2. The key to a child's emotional development is his feeling of being loved and his feeling of emotional security, i.e., emotional warmth.
3. Therefore, a parent should do the following.
   a) Not "tell a child you don't love him."
   b) Show children a great deal of affection.
   c) Use praise as a technique of control.
   d) Cultivate his own emotional security, because parental problems make children insecure.

The idea, which in parody could be called the thermodynamic theory of emotional development, appears obvious, partly because we are steeped in a culture which endorses it. To a geneticist, sociologist, or experimental psychologist, however, it is not so obvious, and to a previous generation of parents trained to believe that specific techniques of feeding, discipline, and toilet-training were crucial, the idea might appear odd.

How do the experts feel about these ideas? Nunnally's experts did not rate the constituent items, except that they slightly favor the idea that deprivation of affection in childhood leads to high adult need to deprive one's own children. However, THE expert endorses it. Dr. Benjamin Spock (1946, p. 3, italics added) begins his book as follows.

One mother tells you you must use the black kind of nipples, another says the yellow. You hear that a baby must be handled as little as possible, that a baby must be cuddled plenty . . . *that fairy tales make children nervous, and that fairy tales are a wholesome outlet.*

Don't take too seriously all that the neighbors say. Don't be overawed by what the experts say. . . . We know for a fact that the *natural loving care* that *kindly* parents give to their children is a hundred times more valuable than their knowing how to pin a diaper on just right, or making a formula expertly. Every time you pick your baby up, even if you do it a little awkwardly at first, every time you change him, bathe him, feed him, *smile* at him, he's getting a feeling that *he belongs to you and that you belong to him.*

Undoubtedly, similar quotations could be chosen from equally eminent authorities, but evidence indicates that Dr. Spock is an especially salient figure in American life. In 1955 Boek *et al.* (1957), interviewing a reasonably heterogeneous (but non-probability) sample of 1,433 new mothers in upstate New York, found 40 per cent citing Spock's *Baby and Child Care* as "especially helpful," with a range from 56 per cent in the highest socio-economic status stratum to 21 per cent in the lowest. Any book which has reached 21 per cent of the mothers in the lowest class in this country is a phenomenon to consider seriously. Whether Spock has changed Americans' ideas or whether Americans read Spock because he fits their ideas, the acceptance of his book provides circumstantial evidence that this doctrine is accepted beyond Nunnally's Champaign sample.

CONCLUSION 8
It appears that the belief that warmth and affection are more important in child-rearing than specific techniques is the single most widely accepted mental health principle in contemporary America.

Correlates of Acceptance

Because parental beliefs have been studied so little in comparison with parental practices, it is very difficult to cite research evidence on differential acceptance of mental health principles of child-rearing. Three studies, however, do shed some oblique light on the problem.

In a superb piece of scholarly detective work, Bronfenbrenner (1958, pp. 424–25) has provided a synthesis of a large number of research studies on social class and child-rearing practices. In his article "Socialization and Social Class through Time and Space," after reviewing fifteen quantitative studies reported over twenty-five years, he draws the following conclusions.

A. Trends in infant care
   1. Over the past quarter of a century, American mothers at all social class levels have become more flexible with respect to infant feeding and weaning.
   2. [Regarding] feeding, weaning, and toilet training. . . . From about 1930 till the end of World War II, the working-class mothers were uniformly more permissive than those of the middle class. . . . After World War II, however, there has been a definite reversal in direction: now it is the middle-class mother who is the more permissive in each of the above areas.
   3. Shifts in the pattern of infant care—especially on the part of middle-class mothers—show a striking correspondence to the changes in practices advocated in successive editions of U.S. Children's Bureau bulletins and similar sources of expert opinion.
B. Trends in child training
   6. Middle-class mothers, especially in the postwar period, [are] consistently more permissive toward the child's expressed needs and wishes.
   7. The middle-class parent, throughout the period covered by this survey, has higher expectations for the child.
   9. Parent-child relationships in the middle class are consistently reported as more acceptant and equalitarian. . . . Within this context the middle class has shown a shift away from the emotional control toward freer expression of affection and greater tolerance of the child's impulses and desires.

In sum, Bronfenbrenner is saying that (1) child training practices are heavily influenced by the better publicized experts; (2) middle-class parents are more exposed to the experts, and their practices shift before those of lower-class parents; and (3) the current trend is toward "permissiveness" and the thermodynamic theory. Drawing on Bronfenbrenner and the previously reviewed materials on beliefs about adjustment, we can suggest the following conclusion.

CONCLUSION 9

Indirect evidence from studies of beliefs about child-rearing suggests that group differences in these beliefs are more a function of differential exposure to "conventional authority" than subcultural differences in values or beliefs.

This line of argument, although indirect, has great importance for mental health education, for it suggests that the task of mental health education is not to wear down existing prejudices and sub-cultural beliefs but rather to reach people who, by and large, are willing and eager to learn. It must be stressed (and Chap. 4 will treat this problem in some detail) that beliefs are not the same as practices, but the general trend of the evidence, across groups and over time, is that the general population is consistently pulled toward the positions advocated by authorities.

At the same time, the thermodynamic theory presents some special problems for the mental health educator. Ignoring tem-porarily whether the theory is correct and justified by scientific evidence, if it is true any attempts to facilitate its acceptance may present special challenges. The point is simply that the expres-sion of affection may not be subject to the same voluntary control as beliefs about weaning, demand feeding, reading techniques, and toilet-training.

The closest we came to statistical evidence on the correlates of warmth comes from two survey studies of child-rearing tech-niques. Sears *et al.* (1957), whose rating scales were discussed earlier, included as one of their scales "Affectionate Relation-ship (Warmth) Mother Child," reporting an inter-rater correla-tion of .533, which we saw to be typical of their ratings for psychological dimensions. No complete data matrices are reported, but two lines of evidence on correlates of warmth can be pieced together.

In the first place, in contrast to a number (but not all) of child-rearing practices, "Warmth" shows a low correlation (.11) with "Mother's Education" (Sears *et al.*, 1957, p. 532). Of thirty-six practices whose correlations are reported, only seven show lower correlations with education, while "Sex Permissiveness," "Permissiveness for Aggression toward Parents," "Lack of Punishment for Aggression toward Parents," and "Lack of Use of Physical Punishment" show correlations of .25 or more with "Education," in line with Bronfenbrenner's analysis (no coincidence, for Bronfenbrenner relies heavily on this study). In the second place, "Warmth" shows correlations with dimensions suggestive of psychological adjustment: "Mother Self-esteem" (.39), "Mother's Evaluation of Father" (.31), "Dissatisfaction with Current Situation" (−.27).

This is not to say that "Warmth" is independent of specific child-rearing techniques. Scattered throughout the book are a number of correlations between the "Warmth" scale and specific practices: "Severity of Toilet-training" (−.30), "Tolerance of Dependence" (.37), "Sex Permissiveness" ("between .21 and .39 for various items"), "Physical Punishment" (−.26), "Severity of Punishment for Aggression" (−.22).

Table 2.13 Intercorrelations of Fels Scales

Scales	Affectionateness	Adjustment	Restrictiveness
Discord* in the home: General atmosphere of conflict, discord, recrimination	+.58	+.64	−.50
Affectionateness		+.44	−.49
Adjustment: General internal adjustment of family, its stability, satisfaction, and happiness			−.36
Restrictiveness of regulations: Restrictiveness and severity of standards to which child is expected to conform			

* Signs of correlations with "Discord" are reversed.

While not independent of other aspects of parental practices, the scattered data reported do suggest that, relatively speaking, warmth is less easily learned from a book than, say, demand feeding. This suggestion is reinforced by findings from the Fels research (Baldwin *et al.*, 1945). The authors report the intercorrelations of thirty rating scales quite similar to those of Sears *et al.* (1957), although no relationships with outside variables are considered. The data come from a longitudinal study of 150 children recruited from the area surrounding Yellow Springs, Ohio, and are based on the ratings of fieldworkers who made twice-yearly visits to their homes. One of the scales is "Affectionateness: The Parents' Expression of Affection to the Child," which at least sounds like warmth. Table 2.13 gives selected intercorrelations. In these data too, the expression of affection appears to be correlated with general family adjustment, although not independent of dimensions of practice.

CONCLUSION 10
Although the evidence is discouragingly fragmentary, it suggests that warmth, as a dimension of parental practice, is less subject to deliberate control and more related to parental adjustment, when compared with other techniques and practices.

RECOMMENDATION 5
To the extent that mental health educators are willing to consider advocating "warmth" as an important aspect of parental practice, research should be instituted to determine (*a*) reliable and valid measures of this variable, (*b*) its distribution in the general population, and (*c*) the degree to which it can be modified.

SUMMARY AND CONCLUSIONS
Having reviewed in some detail subjective and objective measures of mental health, beliefs about adult adjustment, and beliefs about child-rearing—the key variables in the chain of assumptions which underlie mental health education—it is not necessary to review the review. For the reader's convenience, however, we shall repeat in capsule form the conclusions and recommendations set forth in this chapter.

CONCLUSIONS

Adult Mental Health

1. In the general population, individuals vary within a dimension of generalized subjective distress.
2. The reliability of experts' ratings of mental health, while low, is no worse than other behavioral-science ratings.
3. Measures of mental health, using existing techniques, are meaningful only for assessing relative differences between subgroups, not absolute levels.
4. There is no research evidence for or against the assumption that mental illness is the extreme form of the phenomenon we have called generalized subjective distress.

Acceptance of Principles: Adult Adjustment

5. The average man rejects the superstitions and obvious misconceptions about mental health, but he is uniformed and tends to ignore in concrete practice the principles he accepts in theory. He accepts the idea that environmental stress leads to mental illness, but he has few firm opinions on predisposing factors.
6. While the experts are in fair agreement on fallacies of mental health, they have no set of practical, positive actions to recommend to the general population regarding personal adjustment and prevention of mental illness.
7. The general effect of information flow in the United States is to increase the agreement between the population and mental health experts, and those persons most exposed to information show the greatest agreement.

Acceptance of Principles: Child Development

8. It appears that the belief that warmth and affection are more important in child-rearing than specific techniques is the single most widely accepted mental health principle in contemporary America.
9. Although the evidence is discouragingly fragmentary, it suggests that warmth, as a dimension of parental practice, is less subject to deliberate control and more related to parental adjustment, when compared with other techniques and practices.

RECOMMENDATIONS

1. Research on generalized subjective distress should use multiple-item scales, rather than a single indicator, but analysis should be conducted on individual items as well as total scores.

2. Technical research using available interview protocols on representative populations should be conducted, in order to develop rating procedures for assessing mental health.
3. Research using expert raters should use the pooled ratings of two or more raters.
4. High priority should be given to longitudinal studies of the relationship between generalized subjective distress and mental illness.
5. To the extent that mental health educators are willing to advocate "warmth" as an important aspect of parental practice, research should be instituted to determine (*a*) reliable and valid measures of this variable, (*b*) its distribution in the general population, and (*c*) the degree to which it is amenable to modification.

3

Existing Knowledge: Relationships between Variables

Having reviewed a number of studies dealing with the assessment of adult mental health and the general population's beliefs about mental hygiene, we now turn to research regarding the assumed relationships between these variables. In effect we are asking what research has shown regarding the arrows drawn in the diagram of mental health assumptions (see p. 4). We shall follow our pattern of considering first adult mental health and then problems of child development.

ADULT MENTAL HEALTH

Acceptance of Principles and Adult Mental Health
Our search of published literature did not uncover a single study bearing directly on the assumed relationship between a person's acceptance of principles of mental health and his own adjustment, although one or two experimental studies reviewed in the next chapter cast some light on the question.

Although the assumption that acceptance of correct principles leads to improved adult mental health is probably the most important assumption in the set, it has the least firm research foundation. Perhaps it seems so "obvious" that attention has been concentrated on other tasks, or perhaps the research fraternity has so little faith in the efficacy of ideas that it does not consider the question worth studying. Regardless of the reason, we have no direct evidence for or against the proposition. The ideal technique would be to conduct experimental studies in which information was disseminated and changes in understanding and mental health were then measured, but it would still be extremely useful to know if there is even a cross-sectional correlation.

RECOMMENDATION 6

An attempt should be made to determine whether there is a correlation between individuals' mental health and their acceptance of principles of mental hygiene. Because age and education are presumably correlated with both of these variables, it is important that such a study be conducted on a large and heterogeneous population so that their effects can be controlled.

Environmental Correlates of Adult Mental Health

As we have seen, both the general population and the experts accept the idea that mental health is not hereditary, as is color blindness, but is influenced by both present and past experiences. On the relative contribution of current and past events there is less consensus, but everybody believes that under sufficient provocation, the "best adjusted" person will develop symptoms of generalized distress.

From the viewpoint of mental health education, studies showing relationships between environment and mental health have a double importance. On the one hand, they provide documentation for the principle of environmental pressures, and on the other, they provide clues to which target populations are most in need of aid. There is a vast literature on this topic, and we shall not be able to cover it in much detail. However, by collating the outstanding researches we can derive a number of generalizations which have considerable research support.

When one speaks about environmental factors in mental health, it is clear that "environment" is used to describe two rather different phenomena. On the one hand, one would include under "environment" such isolated external events as bereavement, physical illness, job changes, etc., which are assumed to have an impact on a person's mental health. On the other hand, the same term can be used to refer, not to specific events, but to long-term continuing situations which facilitate or interfere with mental health. Thus we shall see that mental health experts tend to believe that there is a sex difference in mental health, not because women are more often exposed to risks of particular crises, but because they are assumed to be continuously subjected to strains which are conducive to mental health problems. While the distinction between crisis and strain is an interesting one, it should not be pushed too hard, for the line is blurry — a long-term stress situation may be merely a long series of small "crises." More important, the research we uncovered bears almost entirely on the situational rather than the event-oriented approach.

We found only one study showing a relationship between a particular external event and mental health, and although the relationship was a strong one, it had little applicability to the problems of Pennsylvania Mental Health, Inc. In researches of *The American Soldier* it was shown quite clearly that exposure to combat in World War II was associated with a lowering of scores on the Neuropsychiatric Screening Adjunct. Star (1949*b*, p. 445) says the following.

If it is difficult to draw conclusions about the effects of overseas service in general, the same is not true about the effects of actual combat. There can be no doubt about the high level of anxiety symptoms among combat troops, both on the ground and in the air.

In a very detailed analysis, Star showed that the combat effect could not be explained by differences in background characteristics. She stated further (Star, 1949*b*, pp. 447 – 48) the following.

In general, the closer men approached to combat, the more likely they were to experience fear reactions . . . men who had undergone air raids or buzz bomb attacks in Europe were more often subject to psychosomatic symptoms than men who had no personal experience with enemy fire. Men who had been subjected to close range enemy fire — rifle fire, mortars, artillery — indicated a somewhat higher level of disturbance, while men who had been in actual combat were, of course, most likely to have these emotional reactions.

At the risk of laboring the obvious, note that these findings provide a fundamental documentation for the environmental assumption. It is clear that regardless of a man's general capacity for adjustment, gross traumatic stress produces a lowering of his mental health status. What may be less obvious, however, is that when we return to these data later in the chapter, we will show that the effects of combat are less than the effects of some of the normal demographic factors to be reviewed.

Having examined this striking but somewhat unusual set of data, we turn our attention away from specific events to findings on long-term situations associated with mental health. We consider first the so-called demographic correlates and then more specific social relationships.

Demographic factors: sex, socio-economic status, and age. — Sex, socio-economic status, and age can be considered "environmental" factors only at a high level of abstraction, where they are interpreted as indicators of differences in patterns of life and hence of stress situations. But since they are the most thoroughly studied variables in the literature, and because some definite relationships turn up, they repay us for our attention, albeit at the price of difficulties in interpretation of the findings.

Sex. Even though women conspicuously outlive men, there is some belief that their mental health states are somewhat poorer. In Nunnally's (1961, p. 74) data, the general public appeared to have little belief in a sex difference, but the experts showed slight support for the propositions on sex difference. In print, the experts are often quite eloquent on this subject, as, for example, the following statement by Bruno Bettelheim, who occupies in the intelligentsia a position much like Dr. Spock's in the general population. Bettelheim, writing in the October, 1962, issue of *Harper's Magazine*, makes the following statement.

The ways in which we bring up many girls in America, and the goals we set for them are so strangely — and often painfully — contradictory that it is only too predictable that their expectations of love and work and marriage should frequently be confused, and that deep satisfactions should elude them.

Professor Bettelheim does not actually come out and say that women are less well adjusted than men (note the innocuous little "many" in the first line, which makes the statement irrefutable), but considering the section headings of his article, "Education for Failure," "Wed to Ceremonial Futility," "Competition in Bed," etc., one can guess his prediction. Of course, his analysis is limited to upper-middle-class women, but we shall return to this particular group before concluding the chapter.

In terms of subjective measures, *Americans View Their Mental Health* provides a definitive answer, being based on a large representative sample, with controls for other variables. Table 3.1 gives Q coefficients between sex and various measures in that study, a positive value indicating that women are more likely to show a given symptom or to be low on a particular index of health. The items are described in the previous chapter. Eight out of the eleven items do show a disadvantage for women — the first of many examples of our previous generalization that, in spite of their positive intercorrelation, different mental health measures give different results. In particular, we note that it is the symptom-like items which give the highest relationships,

Table 3.1 Q Coefficients by Sex, *Americans View Their Mental Health*

Symptom or Health Index	Q
Psychological anxiety (insomnia, nervousness)	+.340
Worry	+.251
Physical anxiety (shortness of breath, heart beating hard)	+.217
Problems raising children	+.206
Physical health (aches and pains, healthy enough)	+.199
Feelings of inadequacy as a parent	+.199
Immobilization (difficulty getting up, hands sweating)	+.195
Experience of problems in marriage	+.185
Marital happiness	+.060
Feelings of marital inadequacy	+.040
Happiness	−.066

while happiness and marital happiness are independent of sex.
Most experts interpret this phenomenon as stemming from
contradictions in sex roles: they assume that, in modern America,
women find it hard to reconcile their wifely duties with their
previous training for achievement and careers. However, data
from *Americans View Their Mental Health* cast some doubt on
this idea. Table 3.2 gives the Q coefficient for the association
between sex and psychological anxiety (the mental health item
with the strongest sex difference) for different age and education
groups. The sex difference is least among young college-graduate
women, who might be expected to show the greatest effects of
cultural pressures, and greatest among grade-school-educated
women and older women of all ages. Thus it is the groups with
the least, not the most, involvement in modern life who show the
sex difference in psychological anxiety.

Table 3.2   Q Coefficients for Sex and Psychological Anxiety

Education	Age		
	21–34	35–54	55 and Over
College High school Grade school	.083 (184) .202 (473) .454 (102)	.149 (200) .360 (511) .330 (292)	.338 (70) .543 (196) .456 (404)

Table 3.3   Q Coefficients for Sex and Mental Health Items, NORC
Survey of Arts and Science Graduate Students

Mental Health Item	Q
Headaches	+.209
Loss of appetite	+.175
Blues	+.172
Insomnia	+.142
Confusion about goals in life	+.101
Low spirits	−.021
Worries about school	−.033
Bad time in graduate school	−.147
Can't force self to work	−.153
Worries about finances	−.156

The NORC survey of arts and science graduate students provides further confirmation for the idea that women's problems of adjustment are not greatest in young, highly educated girls. The Q's between sex and the mental health items from that survey are shown in Table 3.3. As the table demonstrates, there is almost no sex difference here, five items favoring the girls, five favoring the boys. The girls are again high on symptoms. but on indicators of existential malaise such as "Confusion about Goals in Life" there is practically no sex difference.

Shifting from subjective data to experts' ratings, we find that the experts in *Mental Health in the Metropolis* (Srole *et al.*, 1962) do not find any sex difference at all. Calculations from their data give a Q of .051 for psychiatrists' ratings of 657 men and 931 women sampled from Manhattan and rated on mental health. More detailed tabulations show that there was a sex difference among the single respondents, of whom men were rated lower in mental health, but among the married respondents, men held a very slight advantage.

The authors of *Mental Health in the Metropolis* do not report sex differences by education, but they do state that "in the Midtown sample as a whole there are no significant differences between males and females in their mental health composition. This situation persists, we can report, when both age and parental SES are controlled" (Srole *et al.*, 1962, p. 218).

CONCLUSION 11
To the extent that there is a sex difference in mental health, women's adjustment is less favorable, but the relationship is limited to older and less well-educated groups, and expert ratings of impairment show no difference.

Education and socio-economic status. The role of socio-economic status (SES) in mental health has been much studied and has been given particular emphasis with the publication of Hollingshead's (1958) data on treated prevalence in New Haven. For once in our review we are on firm ground, for study after study shows that mental health is positively related to socio-economic status in a variety of measures of mental health and SES.

1. Blood (1960), analyzing a probability sample of 731 wives from Detroit and 178 farm wives from three rural counties close to Detroit, found that marital satisfaction, averaged over a number of content areas, such as standard of living, companionship, understanding, and love and affection, increased strongly with husband's education and slightly with husband's occupation and income.

2. Roth and Peck (1951, p. 479), by rescoring cases in Burgess and Wallin's classic study of marital adjustment according to the Warner status measure, found among 428 husbands and 417 wives (not, however, a representative sample) "an evident trend in the case of both husbands and wives for the marital adjustment score to increase as we move up the social class scale."

3. The *American Soldier* studies showed that in terms of the Neuropsychiatric Screening Adjunct, "the proportion receiving critical scores declined steadily with education" (Star, 1949*a*, p. 420). A similar result was found for scales measuring personal commitment, but a reverse relationship was found for "satisfaction with status and job."

4. The Midtown study produced a rather strong inverse relationship between parental SES and mental health ratings, which persisted when age was controlled (Srole *et al.*, 1962, Chap. 12).

5. Inkeles (1960), in reviewing a number of international surveys, came to the following conclusion.

Taking the available evidence together . . . we cannot entertain any other hypothesis but that the feeling of happiness or of psychic well-being is unevenly distributed in most, perhaps all, countries. Those who are economically well off, those with more education, or whose jobs require more training and skill, more often report themselves happy, joyous, laughing, free of sorrow, satisfied with life's progress. . . . There is, then, good reason to challenge the image of the "carefree but happy poor."

6. By and large, the findings in *Americans View Their Mental Health* give further support to the proposition that mental health is positively associated with SES. But, because data on multiple measures of mental health and different aspects of SES are reported, we may note some qualifications to the general proposi-

Education for Positive Mental Health

tion. Considering education and family income as measures of SES, it appears that the following measures of mental health are related positively to both.

1. Extent of worries[1]
2. Current happiness
3. Marital happiness
4. Job satisfaction (reported for employed men only)
5. Job adequacy (reported for employed men only)
6. Physical Health Symptom Index (all sorts of pains and ailments, healthy enough to carry out things you would like to do)

The relationships with current happiness, shown in Table 3.4, will illustrate the trends found on these items. The better-educated respondents are likely to say that they are "very happy" as contrasted with "pretty happy" or "not too happy" (Gurin *et al.*, 1960). Even more striking, despite the fact that Nunnally's general population sample rejects the idea that money brings happiness, is the relationship (shown in Table 3.5) between income and happiness (Gurin *et al.*, 1960, Tabular Supplement, p. B-2). Furthermore, although they are strongly correlated, Table 3.6 shows that income and education contribute independently to happiness (Gurin *et al.*, 1960, Tabular Supplement, p. B-14).

The pattern of coefficients in Table 3.7 suggests that while both education and income contribute to happiness, the effect of education is somewhat uneven. While very low education (grade

[1] Actually, people in the very small group having an income of $15,000 or more are a little more worried, but over the rest of the range, worries tend to decline as income declines.

Table 3.4 Per Cent "Very Happy," by Education

Education	Per Cent	N
College	43	457
High school	39	1,185
Grade school	23	802

Table 3.5 Per Cent "Very Happy," by Income

Income	Per Cent	N
$15,000 or over	53	66
$10,000–$14,999	48	120
$8,000–$9,999	43	158
$7,000–$7,999	48	141
$6,000–$6,999	46	237
$5,000–$5,999	37	322
$4,000–$4,999	36	390
$3,000–$3,999	31	290
$2,000–$2,999	23	259
$1,000–$1,999	22	207
Under $1,000	20	200

Table 3.6 Per Cent "Very Happy," by Education and Income

Education	Under $5,000		$5,000 and Over	
	Per Cent	N	Per Cent	N
College	35	142	47	305
High school	32	584	46	578
Grade school	22	609	30	158

Table 3.7 Q Coefficients with Happiness in Table 3.6

Coefficient	Group Measured	Value	
Income	Total sample		.338
	College	.244	
	High school	.288	
	Grade school	.206	
Education (college *v.* non-college)	Total sample		.232
	High income	.081	
	Low income	.186	
Education (high school or more *v.* grade school)	Total sample		.357
	High income	.330	
	Low income	.271	

school) is associated with a sharp drop in happiness, the incre-
ment due to college training compared with high school is quite
small. In this sense, low education appears to reduce happiness
more than high education raises it.

For a number of mental health measures, a different picture
emerges. Some items show a reverse relationship, particularly
with education.

1. Feelings of inadequacy as a spouse increase with education
   and have no consistent relationship with income.
2. Reporting of marital problems increases with education and
   shows no consistent relationship with income.
3. Feelings of parental inadequacy increase with education (no
   tabulations are reported for income).
4. Reporting job-related problems increases with education and
   with income.
5. The Immobilization Symptom Score (difficulty getting up in
   the morning, hands damp and clammy) increases strikingly
   with education, but is independent of income.

Finally, two of the symptom indices, "Psychological Anxiety"
(insomnia, nervousness), which showed a striking sex difference, and "Physical Anxiety" (shortness of breath, heart beating
hard) seem to show no consistent relationships with education
and income in the tables where both are presented simultaneously, possibly because the relationship between "Income"
and "Psychological Anxiety" appears to be curvilinear when
"Income" is treated alone. Gurin, Veroff, and Feld interpret
these and similar findings by positing that, while higher SES is
associated with more intrinsic gratifications, and thus with
health and happiness, the greater sensitivity and more "psychological" orientation of the better-educated increases their level
of self-criticism.

7. A rather similar set of findings emerges from Stouffer's
analysis of background differences in adjustment of soldiers in
The American Soldier (Stouffer and DeVinney, 1949), which
stressed content concerns rather than the psychoneurotic symptoms analyzed by Star and noted above. In summarizing a large
number of comparisons, Stouffer concludes that the better-

educated soldiers tended to be higher in personal esprit and personal commitment but lower in satisfaction with status or job and approval of the army (Stouffer and DeVinney, 1949, p. 228), again showing better "adjustment" along with greater criticisms.

Even though the proposition requires qualification when studies reporting multiple and complex tabulations are reviewed, we see no reason to withdraw the general proposition that adult mental health and adjustment are much less favorable in the lower-SES groups, a target population seldom reached by mental health educators. However, it is extremely difficult to draw any firm conclusions on the factors which explain why the finding obtains. The same data can be used to support quite contradictory interpretations.

To begin with the obvious, the lower socio-economic status group lives in an environment which places it under greater pressures, and, regardless of his capacity for adjustment, the lower-SES adult simply has many more environmental threats. In support of this idea is the repeated finding that, when asked directly, Americans say their major worries are in the areas of health and finances, both, of course, strongly correlated with SES.

Stouffer, in a 1954 national sample of Americans twenty-one and older (N = 4,933) and a sample of community leaders (N = 1,500) obtained the results shown in Table 3.8 in answer to the question, "What kinds of things worry you most?"

Table 3.8 Worries of Community Leaders and Cross-Section

Worries	Community Leaders (Per Cent)		Cross-Section (Per Cent)	
Personal or family economic problems	28	44	43	67
Personal and family health problems	16		24	
Other personal and family problems		38		30
World problems including war	22		8	
Communists or civil liberties	5	52	0	14
Other national or local problems	25		6	
Never worry		11		9
Total*		145		120
N		1,500		4,933

* Adds to more than 100 per cent because of multiple answers.

Table 3.8 illustrates the idea rather neatly. The community leaders, who may be assumed to be a high-SES group, report more worries (their answers total 145 per cent, in contrast with 120 per cent for the cross-section), but the cross-section is essentially worried about money and health, while it is the high-SES group that may indulge in the luxury of concerns about the state of the world. Putting it another way, there is a distinct suggestion that concerns about reality may well overshadow other factors as a determinant of generalized subjective distress.

At the same time, some of the same findings may be used to support the idea that education at least represents a permanent capacity to attain a superior level of mental health, regardless of the situation. The most striking example is the clear-cut advantage of the higher-educated soldier over the lower-educated one, even in combat situations, in which the environment is, in a sense, held constant. Consider, for example, the simultaneous effects of education and combat experience on soldiers under twenty-five, as reported in Star's (1949*a*, p. 447) analyses and shown in Table 3.9. The high-school graduates exposed to actual combat have lower anxiety scores than grade-school-level soldiers with no combat experience, which suggests that education taps something more than current life situations.

If SES taps a relatively permanent, rather than a situational, factor in mental health, the possibility arises that SES is the effect of mental health rather than its cause. If, for example, SES differences in current situations had nothing to do with

Table 3.9 Per Cent of Soldiers Receiving Critical Scores on Anxiety Index, by Education and Combat Experience

Education	Combat Experience					
	None		Under Fire		Actual Combat	
	Per Cent	N	Per Cent	N	Per Cent	N
Grade school	40	81	47	111	57	213
Part high school	34	152	42	178	47	351
High school graduate	20	246	29	355	36	500

mental health, but children who were "maladjusted" continued into adult life with low levels of mental health and were less successful in their education and employment, we would still find a correlation between adult SES and mental health. The possibility is not only logically seductive, but one study presents data to support it. In a study to be reviewed in more detail later, Robins *et al.* (1962) compare the occupational mobility of 524 children referred to a municipal psychiatric clinic between 1924 and 1929 with a control group of 100 children selected from public school records, the controls being chosen to have a similar distribution on residence, sex, race, and year of birth. Their striking findings can be summarized (see Table 3.10) by considering the percentage who "rose" and "fell" in occupational status compared with their fathers, after excluding the children of professional and executive fathers (of whom there are only seven control cases).

When compared with control cases, children referred to a behavior clinic were much less likely to move up the SES ladder and much more likely to move down it. Even though the case bases are small, the relationship is statistically significant and suggests that adult SES may be a function of mental health as well as mental health's being a function of adult SES. Robins *et al.* (1962) examined separately the data for patients referred because of antisocial behavior (defined by having a record of

Table 3.10 Occupational Mobility of Ex-patients and Controls at Time of Follow-Up

Father	Unemployed Unskilled	Skilled	Clerical, Small Business
	Per Cent Who Rose		
Controls Patients	83 (18) 49 (186)	63 (30) 27 (59)	50 (28) 20 (93)
	Per Cent Who Fell		
Controls Patients		20 (30) 54 (59)	21 (28) 50 (93)

juvenile-court appearance) and other patients. They show clearly that the difference in mobility is produced by the antisocial group, and, for the remaining patients, mobility patterns of experimental and control subjects are no different.

It is difficult to interpret these findings, even though the statistical differences are clear-cut. If we assume that antisocial behavior belongs with the complex of phenomena we have called mental health, it follows that there is a strong case for concluding that SES is a function of mental health. But, if we assume that only the non-juvenile-delinquent patients had mental health disturbances, then the study must be counted against the belief that SES is the dependent variable. We lean toward the latter position, but we can hardly take a firm stance on the basis of the limited evidence.

The Midtown survey attempts to come to grips with this problem by treating both current and parental SES, but since the authors report their tabulations in a highly elliptical fashion (reporting mental health ratings by current SES and by parental SES, but never by both) it is difficult to draw any conclusion beyond their statement (Srole *et al.*, 1962, p. 235) that the SES difference

also characterized those in the sample's youngest age group, who only recently have crossed the threshold from adolescence. It was thus possible to reject the hypothesis that SES origin differentials in mental health had almost entirely been generated during adult life.

However, the finding does not make it possible to reject the hypothesis that the differential is due to contemporary environmental differences and that the lives of young lower-class people are not much more gratifying than the lives of older lower-class people.

CONCLUSION 12

Numerous studies and findings suggest that adult mental health is more favored in higher socio-economic status groups. However, higher education apparently produces an increased sensitivity and self-critical capacity, which slightly offsets this trend. Also, the available evidence does not enable us to determine how much of this reflects differential environmental pressures, how much reflects a superior adjustment capacity of higher-educated groups, or the extent to which SES is determined by mental health.

Age. Any well-documented findings on the relationship between age and mental health would provide important theoretical information, as well as crucial suggestions for action to take on programs. If mental health were shown to increase with age, one might consider this evidence for the value of teaching adjustment techniques, and he might think of programs for speeding up this process. If, on the contrary, it were shown that mental health decreases with age, one would think in terms of the continuous erosion of mental health capacity and concentrate on programs to prevent this loss. These extremes do not exhaust the possibilities; the relationship may be neither one of increase nor one of decrease but may vary in intensity, decreases occurring in particular ages which constitute crisis or stress points.

By and large, the literature reviewed leans toward the proposition that mental health declines with age, but there are enough exceptions to require considerable qualification of this statement. Let us consider the studies.

1. Blood's survey of Detroit wives (Blood and Wolfe, 1960) leads him to the conclusion that marital adjustment is subject to 'the corrosion of time," and his data do show a decline in his adjustment index with years of marriage and progress in the life cycle. Unfortunately, education, an important correlate of his satisfaction index, is not controlled in these tabulations, and older people tend to have much lower levels of schooling. Therefore, his results cannot be considered unequivocal.

2. The psychiatric ratings in *Mental Health in the Metropolis* (Srole *et al.*, 1962) decline steadily with age in tables controlling for sex and marital status and thus controlling for parental SES. Thus, for example, in married women the per cent rated "Impaired" is 13 for those aged twenty to twenty-nine; 22 for those thirty to thirty-nine; 18 for those forty to forty-nine; and 31 for wives aged fifty to fifty-nine (Srole *et al.*, 1962, p. 178). No data, however, are reported controlling for the respondent's own education or SES because of the author's morbid fear that these are results, not causes, of low adjustment.

Education for Positive Mental Health

3. The analyses by Star (1949*a*) and by Stouffer and De-Vinney (1949) on army adjustment showed—under numerous controls—lower scores for older soldiers on the Neuropsychiatric Screening Adjunct and on "Personal Commitment" but not on "Satisfaction with Status and Job" or "Approval of the Army." Older soldiers, naturally, were still rather young men.

4. Lansing and Morgan (1955) found in a national survey that "Satisfaction with Standard of Living" has a non-linear relationship with life-cycle progress, rising during the early years of marriage, dipping during the years when most of one's children are preschool age, and then rising steadily during the later years. Their analysis suggests that during the early years of marriage expenses rise, but income tends to rise at a faster rate; during the early years of child-bearing, income and expenses continue to rise, but expenses rise faster, creating a peak in personal debt; and in the later years of marriage, after the children are grown, both income and expenses decline, but expenses decline faster, creating a more favorable net position even though incomes in later years are low.

5. *Americans View Their Mental Health* (Gurin *et al.*, 1960), because of its larger number of measures, provides the most complex results. In this national survey some indices increase with age, some decrease with age, and some are independent of age. Table 3.11 presents measures showing declines in unfavor-

Table 3.11 Age and Decline in Per Cent of Unfavorable Responses on Mental Health Indices

Measures	Age					
	21–24	25–34	35–44	45–54	55–64	65 and Over
Marital inadequacy	66	61	53	46	45	35
Marital problems	45	50	42	38	31	19
Parental inadequacy	50		52	44		41
Immobilization (men)	80	77	66	54	44	33
Immobilization (women)	77	73	77	65	59	42

able responses,[2] and Table 3.12 gives measures showing an increase in unfavorable responses. In addition, worries and marital happiness show no clear-cut age trend, while "Physical Anxiety" increases with age in women but not in men. The findings seem to support two separate lines of interpretation, one psychological and one environmental.

Apparently, age is associated with strong differences in psychological perspective. As the authors put it (Gurin *et al.*, 1960, p. 212): "The most consistent difference we obtained between young and old people was the minimization of both self-doubt and the perception of problems among the older respondents." Since this trend is similar to the findings on "Education," and since there are considerable age differences in educational attainment, it is important to note that these differences remain when education is controlled. Table 3.13 presents the data of Gurin *et al.* (1960, p. 108) that demonstrates the trend.

There are a number of explanations we may advance. Gurin *et al.* consider the possibility of a historical increase in psychological sensitivity, i.e., that each new generation is more aware of its problems than was the last, and also the possibility that as age increases there is a lowering of aspirations and expectations, so that the older person sees fewer discrepancies between his situa-

[2] Because the percentages are taken from various tables, the N's vary somewhat due to differences in non-response. The smallest age category consists of somewhat more than 250 cases in the group aged twenty-one to twenty-four.

Table 3.12 Age and Increase in Per Cent Unfavorable on Mental Health Indices

Measures	Age					
	21–24	25–34	35–44	45–54	55–64	65 and Over
Happiness	40		38	34	27	
Physical health (men)	8	8	19	18	32	41
Physical health (women)	12	18	19	26	37	49
Physical anxiety (men)	33	30	44	47	51	59
Physical anxiety (women)	42	49	53	55	65	65

tion and his standards of what is desirable. The latter idea is consistent with Lansing and Morgan's (1955) findings and is much like the concept of disengagement advanced by Cumming and Henry (1961, p. 211) on the basis of a study of older people in Kansas City: "Disengagement is an inevitable process in which many of the relationships between a person and other members of society are severed, and those remaining are altered in quality."

At the same time that aging seems to be associated with a difference in "frame of reference" which reduces certain feelings of distress, it is also associated with generally less favorable environmental settings. The older person is much more often under environmental pressures of a nature that has been shown to lead to subjective distress. Physical illness, breakup of the family unit, and low income can hardly facilitate good spirits, even though cognitive mechanisms may soften their impact. Thus, it is important to note the progressive decrease in happiness in Table 3.13. Part of the difference is undoubtedly due to physical disability, as suggested by the relationships with the somatic indices in Table 3.13. But that is not all there is to the story. Gerald Gurin of the Survey Research Center kindly made available to us the original IBM cards from his study and thus made possible the construction of Table 3.14.

The introduction of an SES index based on income and occupation removes the age difference in happiness. But we must stress that this does not mean the relationship is spurious. It

Table 3.13 Per Cent Reporting Feelings of Inadequacy in Marriage, by Sex, Age, and Education

Sex	Education	Age		
		21−34	35−54	55 and Over
Male	College	65	58	50
	High school	65	45	42
	Grade school	44	55	43
Female	College	78	60	–
	High school	62	55	38
	Grade school	57	37	32

serves rather to explain why the relationship occurs. The lower happiness of the older American is apparently due to his lower socio-economic status.

CONCLUSION 13
Age differences in mental health are complex, although studies tend to show less favorable results for older people. We note two contradictory trends: (1) older people are more often under environmental stresses which increase generalized subjective distress (low SES, physical illness, social isolation); and (2) older people apparently are more likely to have a "frame of reference" which softens the negative impact of environmental stresses.

Social relationships.—Turning from the generalized demographic variables of sex, SES, and age to consider more specific social relationships as factors in mental health, we avoid some of the problems of interpreting the meaning of the findings, but unfortunately we also run into an area in which there are many fewer studies. We shall review four topics: community differences, marital relationships, peer relationships, and religion.

Community differences. Although "community studies" play a large part in the research on mental health, they are typically studies within a given community, rather than comparisons between communities. Thus, although one might expect that com-

Table 3.14 Per Cent "Very Happy," by Age, Education, and Income

Education*	Income†	Age		
		21–34	35–54	55 and Over
Total		40 (749)	36 (974)	27 (632)
High High	High Low	49 (332)	44 (447)	46 (97)
Low	High	36 (332)	35 (323)	24 (221)
Low	Low	20 (85)	21 (204)	23 (314)

*High education: high school or beyond.
†High income: $5,000 or more.

munity differences in mental health would be a major research topic, the only source of information we could find on this topic is *Americans View Their Mental Health.* Remembering that Nunnally's general population showed some signs of believing that large cities have an adverse effect on mental health, and noting that it is fashionable these days for the intelligentsia to decry the emotional stresses of living in the suburbs, let us examine the data on city size.

Gurin *et al.* (1960, pp. 221–30) minimize the differences in community size with the following statement.

> Only four sets of findings suggested enough of a difference for inclusion in tables, and these are far from striking. . . . The general picture that emerges is one of minimal relationship between place of residence and the kinds of feelings of adjustment that we have measured. Furthermore, regional differences (South, Northeast, Midwest, Far West) also did not emerge from the data.

For the data which are reported, a rough pattern does emerge. In Table 3.15, rather than present the percentage figures, we rank the city types using 1 for the highest symptom level and 5 for the lowest. At the end of each row we have indicated the Q measure

Table 3.15 Summary of Relationships between Mental Health Indices and City Size

Measure	City Type					Q, Ranks 1 and 5
	Metropolitan	Suburb	Small City	Small Town	Rural	
Physical health (men)	2.5	5	2.5	4	1	.373
Worries	1	5	3.5	3.5	2	.297
Psychological anxiety (women)	1	5	4	3	2	.269
Physical health (women)	1	5	4	2	3	.256
Immobilization (men)	5	4	1	3	2	.221
Unhappiness	1	5	2	3.5	3.5	.200
Psychological anxiety (men)	2.5	4	2.3	5	1	.179
Immobilization (women)	3.5	1.5	5	3.5	1.5	.092
Average rank	2.2	4.3	3.0	3.4	2.0	

Source: Gurin *et al.* (1960, Tabular Supplement, pp. B–40, B–42.)

of association between the rank-1 and rank-5 types, which is the largest possible association of the ten possible contrasts.

To begin with, for the few items that do show a difference, the Q's even between the extremes are quite small. However, a slight pattern emerges which manages to refute the general population and the literati at one time. Both rural areas and metropolitan centers tend to show lower levels of mental health where there are differences, and suburbs come off the best. Although the book presents no tabulations that justify the inference, our assumption is that SES explains even this weak pattern, since rural areas and the centers of large cities have high concentrations of lower-SES groups, while suburbs tend to be relatively high-SES areas.

CONCLUSION 14
Community differences in size and urbanization are relatively unimportant to generalized subjective distress.

Marital relationships. For behavioral-science research to document the fact that marital status is related to mental health would be merely another attempt to belabor a truism, except for the fact that the relationship is difficult to document. By and large, the evidence is that married adults are superior in mental health to single adults, but enough exceptions occur that someone from Missouri may well wish to leave the question open. Four studies present appropriate data.

1. Tables in *Mental Health in the Metropolis* controlling for age and sex show that mental health ratings differ by marital status as follows: (*a*) among men, the married received the most favorable ratings, the single, the next most favorable, and the divorced, the least favorable (there were not enough widowed men to justify tabulations); (*b*) among women, divorcees received lower ratings, but differences between single, married, and widowed are not consistent in the age groups (Srole *et al.*, 1962, Chap. 10).

2. The NORC survey of graduate students showed that, for four of the mental health items ("Loss of Appetite," "Insomnia," "Blues," and "Confusion about Goals in Life"), married students

had more favorable self-ratings: Q's for each of these items were greater than .15. There was no item on which married graduate students had a negative relationship of .15 or greater. However, we have seen that, except for goal confusion, these items are relatively "masculine," and many more of the married students are men (women drop out of graduate school when they get married). Thus, tabulations holding sex constant would reduce or eliminate these small relationships.

3. Stouffer and DeVinney (1949, p. 228), in analyzing adjustment of soldiers in World War II, concluded—after quite elaborate tabulations holding constant a number of other variables—that married soldiers were *lower* in "Personal Esprit" and "Personal Commitment," but marital status had no consistent effect on "Satisfaction with Status or Job" or with "Approval or Criticism of the Army." These negative findings cannot really be compared with the other studies, since they involve not the effect of marital status but the effect of being removed temporarily from a marital status and, seen in this light, suggest that the presence of a spouse *adds* to adjustment.

4. Gurin *et al.* (1960, pp. 230–38) report only one really important difference by marital status: married adults are considerably more likely to report themselves very happy (36 per cent of the men and 43 per cent of the women, in contrast with 26 per cent or less in each of the single, widowed, or divorced groups of each sex). None of their other measures showed a consistent relationship with marital status within each sex, except that the widowed of either sex were high on "Worries" and low on "Immobilization."

The IBM cards lent by the Survey Research Center allowed us to proceed a step beyond the analysis reported by Gurin *et al.* and to examine the relationship between marriage and happiness, holding age and SES constant. Our findings are given in Table 3.16. The effects of SES and marital status are independent and similar in each age group, producing a range in the per cent "Very Happy" of from 49 among the high-status married to 16 among the low-status non-married. Again we see that age in itself is unrelated to happiness when SES and marital status are controlled, which underlines our previous conclusion that the lower levels of happiness among older Americans stem from their less gratifying environments, not from an erosion of their capacities for adjustment. Furthermore, the effect of marital status is considerable. In each age category, married people at the lowest SES level are as likely to be happy as non-married people at the highest SES level. Considerable residual variation remains even after SES and marital status are controlled, but these are clearly the two most important correlates of happiness of all the background variables.

A NOTE ON RACE AND HAPPINESS

Although there are too few studies of race differences in mental health to justify separate treatment of the topic, the Survey Research Center data made it possible to examine Negro-white differences in happiness. The cultural stereotype of the happy-go-lucky Negro freed

Per Cent "Happy," by Race

	Race	Per Cent "Happy"	N
	White	36	2,163
	Negro	22	188

Table 3.16 Marital Status and Per Cent "Very Happy," Controlling for Age and Socio-economic Status

Married	Income*	Education*	Age			
			21–34	35–54	55 and Over	Total
Yes	High	High	52 (299)	47 (400)	54 (72)	49 (771)
	High⎱ Low⎰	Low⎱ High⎰	40 (268)	38 (257)	29 (121)	37 (646)
	Low	Low	23 (66)	24 (153)	27 (176)	25 (395)
No	High	High	24 (33)	19 (47)	24 (25)	22 (105)
	High⎱ Low⎰	Low⎱ High⎰	19 (64)	23 (66)	17 (101)	19 (230)
	Low	Low	11 (19)	12 (51)	19 (138)	16 (208)

*SES index is defined as in Table 3.14.

from the onerous burdens of first-class citizenship receives little corroboration from the tables we ran. Over all, Negroes are considerably less likely to say they are very happy, as we see in the first of the accompanying tabulations.

Because of the extreme SES differences in race (42 per cent of the Negroes reported incomes under $2,000 in comparison with 15 per cent of the whites in the SRC sample) it is necessary to control for this difference. The results are given in the second of the accompanying tabulations. In the lowest-income group the race difference in happiness is slight, but at the higher-income levels the difference is considerable. Certainly some of the greater unhappiness of Negro Americans can be explained by their low incomes, but income differences do not provide a total explanation.

When we turn to marital status (41 per cent of the adult Negroes were not married, in contrast with 22 per cent of the whites) the case bases become very small, and the results, given in the third of the tabulations herewith, are somewhat complicated.

Among the married, our original relationships all hold. Whites are more likely to consider themselves happy, regardless of income level, and happiness is more common in the higher-income group of either race. Among the non-married, however, the race difference disappears, as

Per Cent "Happy," by Race and Income

Income	Whites	Negroes
Under $2,000	22 (308)	18 (78)
$2,000–$3,999	29 (461)	23 (66)
$4,000 or more	42 (1,333)	30 (40)

Per Cent "Happy," by Race, Income, and Marital Status

Income	Married		Not Married	
	White	Negro	White	Negro
Under $2,000	30 (136)	11 (37)	16 (172)	24 (41)
$2,000–$3,999	32 (324)	24 (42)	21 (137)	21 (24)
$4,000 or more	45 (1,177)	30 (30)	19 (156)	30 (10)
Total	41 (1,637)	21 (109)	18 (465)	24 (75)

does the income difference, which was quite slight but present among the non-married in Table 3.16. Two quite different interpretations may be advanced. One possibility is that, among the non-married, background factors such as SES and race make little or no difference in happiness, while among the married, race and income are important factors. An alternative possibility, however, is that marital status has no correlation with happiness among Negroes. Since common-law unions and casual relationships are much more common among Negroes, possibly more of the "Not Married" Negroes are actually receiving the emotional support from a continued relationship and belong in the "Married" column. Another possibility is that, because of the disadvantaged position of Negroes, marriage confers more problems than gratifications upon them and the levels of happiness of married Negroes are unduly depressed. The data are too scanty to allow us to pursue the analysis further, but the general point, the decrease in happiness of Negroes, follows from either interpretation. The difference is whether we assume that race affects happiness directly or, by affecting the nature of marriage, indirectly.

CONCLUSION 15
The evidence on marital status and mental health is inconsistent, although more often than not it suggests superior adjustment for the married person.

If it is unclear whether the existence of a spouse is conducive to favorable mental health status, it is crystal clear that the relation to one's spouse is a key aspect of mental health in the adult population (of which over 80 per cent of those aged thirty to sixty-four are married). We have already seen that marital happiness is the one consistent correlate of overall happiness in the indices used in *Americans View Their Mental Health*, and many definitions of mental health include marital adjustment by fiat.

Our intent is not to review here the voluminous literature on marital adjustment but merely to note its importance. But to indicate the general trend of the findings, it may be well to sketch Blood's major conclusions, since his probability sample of Detroit wives is probably the best and most recent data on the subject. At the end of his book, Blood (1960, p. 252) summarizes the correlates of his marital adjustment index as follows.

The major sources of strength in marriage . . . are four: (1) the family's social status; (2) the couple's homogamy; (3) the extent to which they meet each others' needs; and (4) children — in moderation. Against these must be set a counter-agent; the corrosion of time.

We have already reviewed his SES and age data, but homogamy and number of children deserve a little further elaboration. By homogamy, Blood means simply similarity between the spouses in social characteristics, a factor generally noted in this type of research. Blood shows that his measure of marital adjustment declines when there is (*a*) a marked difference in age between the spouses, (*b*) a marked difference in education, or (*c*) an intermarriage of religions. His plea for moderation in number of children stems from the fact that his index of adjustment increases from zero to three children but declines when there are four and five. Since SES is not controlled in his tabulations, we cannot be sure that number of children is an independent factor, although the idea is intuitively attractive.

Peer relationships. One of the most commonly accepted principles of sociology is the idea that being imbedded in a mesh of close interpersonal ties ("social cohesiveness," "primary group relations," "social support," "sociometric status") is conducive to favorable psychological states, much akin to what we have defined as mental health. Like many powerful ideas, it has seldom been put directly to the test of research. Rather, the principle is frequently used to explain observed correlations between other variables. For example, the relatively high deviance rates (crime, psychosis, alcoholism, suicide, etc.) in urban areas with high rates of spatial mobility[3] have often been interpreted in terms of the lowering of adjustment associated with the loosening of social bonds.

We were able to find only three studies which consider a direct correlation between interpersonal relationships and mental health. Of the three, two are cross-sectional studies, which means they are open to the charge that the interpersonal relationship

[3] Actually, the question whether mobility rates correlate with deviance independently or only because of the low SES of these areas is currently under strong debate in sociology.

may stem from adjustment, rather than vice versa. The third, however, is an intriguing longitudinal study which does suggest that interpersonal environments are associated with changes in mental health.

The first is the NORC survey of graduate students. In the book reporting on that study (Davis, 1962, p. 244), peer-group membership is used as a control variable in a table assessing the effect of financial worries on morale. We can rearrange the table to show a slight but consistent relationship between subjective distress and peer-group membership, controlling for marital status, concern about grades, and financial worries. The variables are the following.

1. *Peer-group membership* Students were asked about the existence of informal groups in their departments. "Yes" indicates students who say such groups exist and that they are members, "no" means either students who say no groups exist or that they are not members of a group.
2. *Financial worry* Students were asked how much they worried about their *immediate* financial situation.
3. *Concern about grades* Answer to question about degree of satisfaction with grades. "High" indicates very or fairly dissatisfied; "low," very or fairly satisfied.
4. *Marital status* Married versus single and ex-married.
5. *Morale* Index based on a combination of the "Spirits" and "Good Time in Graduate School" items described in Chapter 2.

Over a range of stress situations (from worry about both grades and finances to worry about neither) and among single and married students, the peer-group member tends to have higher morale. Furthermore, the marital-status effect noted above is independent, so that the two social relationships have a cumulative effect. For example, among the students with concerns about grades and finances who are high on the morale index, 50 per cent are married and belong to a peer group, 40 per cent are married or peer-group members but not both, and 29 per cent have neither source of social support.

Table 3.17 suggests that social support has a positive effect on mental health as defined here. It is, of course, entirely possible that the causal direction is reversed and that the correlation is due to a tendency for students with adjustment problems to be less attractive to their peers. William Erbe of the State University of Iowa has been engaged in an intensive analysis of the NORC data on graduate-student peer-group membership, and in a memorandum now being prepared for publication, he concludes that group membership is largely a function of "accessibility" rather than personal characteristics. That is, students who have jobs and housing situations which throw them in with other students tend to be group members regardless of their personal characteristics, while students whose orbits lead them away from campus are seldom group members—an illustration of George Homans' principle that "interaction leads to liking." Erbe's results constitute circumstantial evidence that the relationship in Table 3.17 is not a spurious function of membership selection, but the issue cannot be put to a definite test with these data.

While the graduate-student study suggests that the quantity of peer social relationships has an effect on mental health, a recent stimulating study by Rosenberg (1962) suggests that the quality of the relationship is important. Rosenberg collected self-administered questionnaires from approximately 1,000 New York

Table 3.17 Per Cent of Graduate Students High on Morale Index, by Marital Status and Peer-Group Membership

Concern About:		Married	Group Member		Yes − No	Q
Grades	Finances		No	Yes		
High	High	No	29 (45)	40 (54)	+11	.240
High	High	Yes	40 (56)	50 (48)	+10	.200
High	Low	No	47 (95)	53 (88)	+ 6	.120
High	Low	Yes	59 (69)	65 (60)	+ 6	.127
Low	High	No	46 (66)	49 (82)	+ 3	.060
Low	High	Yes	55 (103)	55 (88)	0	.000
Low	Low	No	62 (193)	64 (212)	+ 2	.043
Low	Low	Yes	71 (204)	77 (212)	+ 6	.155

State high-school juniors and seniors in ten public high schools, the total group constituting a probability sample of public high-school upperclassmen in New York State. After being asked their own religion the students were questioned on the following: "Think back to the time when you were in grammar school. Generally speaking, what was the religious affiliation of most of the people in the neighborhood in which you lived?" It was thus possible to classify the students, not only on their own religion, but also by whether they were in a religious majority or minority in their neighborhood. Using three separate and familiar measures of mental health (a scale of self-esteem, a psychosomatic-symptoms scale based on the Neuropsychiatric Screening Adjunct, and a scale of depressive affect)[4] Rosenberg shows a consistent association between "dissonant religious contexts" and low mental health. Table 3.18 illustrates his findings.

The average of the nine Q coefficients (.21) indicates a small but consistent effect—a tendency for high-school students who

[4]Sample items from the self-esteem scale are: "At times I think I am no good at all," "I take a positive attitude toward myself," "I feel I do not have much to be proud of." Sample items from the depressive affect scale are: "On the whole, how happy would you say you are?" "In general, how would you say you feel most of the time—in good spirits or in low spirits?" "I get a lot of fun out of life."

Table 3.18 Per Cent with Low Scores on Mental Health Indices, by Religion and Dissonance of Religious Context

Measure	Student's Religion	Neighborhood Same or Mixed	Neighborhood Chiefly Different	Difference	Q
Low self-esteem	Protestant	25 (241)	31 (164)	+ 6	.148
	Catholic	29 (458)	41 (37)	+12	.260
	Jewish	18 (80)	29 (41)	+11	.300
Symptoms	Protestant	48 (245)	54 (164)	+ 5	.120
	Catholic	55 (467)	65 (37)	+10	.206
	Jewish	51 (77)	55 (42)	+ 4	.080
Depressive affect	Protestant	11 (221)	22 (148)	+11	.391
	Catholic	18 (429)	20 (35)	+ 2	.065
	Jewish	16 (70)	28 (39)	+12	.342

grew up in neighborhoods where they were members of a religious minority to be lower in mental health. Rosenberg interprets the findings in two ways. First, he shows that reported experiences of prejudice are related both to dissonant religious context and to lowered mental health, suggesting an obvious explanation. However, when reported experience of prejudice is controlled, the original relationship does not appear, which leads Rosenberg (1962, p. 9) to state the following.

But it is probably more than simple prejudice, narrowly conceived as hostility to members of a group, which is responsible for these results. Beyond this, actual cultural dissimilarity may produce rejection . . . qualities which may be accepted or admired in one's own group may be rejected by members of another group. Hence, there is a real likelihood that one will feel different when in a dissonant social context, and this sense of difference may lead the individual to question himself, doubt himself, wonder whether he is unworthy.

The suggestion of Rosenberg's study, therefore, is that the quality of social contacts is important as well as the quantity, and that it is interaction with people who are essentially similar in values which improves mental health. Since "normal" interaction tends to be with people who are essentially similar (note that in Table 3.18 the bulk of students, regardless of religion, reported growing up in neighborhoods of coreligionists or in "mixed" neighborhoods) one can expect a high rate of social interaction to be generally associated with mental health. But when interaction is chiefly with hostile persons or persons having rather different values, the prediction would be that high rates of social interaction would be associated with lower mental health.[5]

This general idea is given further support in the third research report, a longitudinal study by Fiedler *et al.* (1959). The study has already been described in Chapter 2, where data on associations among mental health measures were discussed. We said in Chapter 2 that mental health measures were collected on two

[5]The idea that people prefer others who have similar attitudes and values is the heart of the "theory of structural balance," as set forth by Fritz Heider, Dorwin Cartwright and Frank Harary, and others. A number of propositions which follow from this idea are summarized in a paper by Davis (1963).

samples of college men and on two samples of soldiers, and the instruments were repeated after an interval ranging from six weeks to three months, depending on the sample.

The independent variable, "Assumed Similarity," has been studied at length by Fiedler and his associates and comes down to perceptions of similarity and difference among members of a group. However, its operational definition is difficult to put into words and can best be conveyed by an example. Consider a four-person group in which each member is asked to rate himself and the three other members on a given dimension. Sixteen observations are produced, as shown by the accompanying tabulation. A rating of 31 is subject 3's rating of subject 1; a rating of 44 is subject 4's self-rating, etc. Two types of discrepancies can be examined regarding a particular person. First, by looking across each row, one can compare the diagonal (self-) rating with the other ratings to compute the perceived similarity between each person and the group. This is called $\overline{AS}_g$ or "average similarity which subject assumes between himself and other members of his group." Second, by looking down each column, one can compare the discrepancy between the column entry and the diagonal entry in that row and compute the perceived similarity between the group and the person. This is called $\overline{AS}_s$ or "group members' average similarity to the subject — the extent to which subject is accepted by others in his group."

Common sense would tell us that the two scores should be strongly correlated; if people think they are different from the group, group members should agree. But in each of his four samples Fiedler found that, while internal consistency was high (discrepancies tended to be similar across the dimensions rated for both $\overline{AS}_g$ and $\overline{AS}_s$), the two indices were essentially independent

Rater	Ratee			
	1	2	3	4
1	11	12	13	14
2	21	22	23	24
3	31	32	33	34
4	41	42	43	44

when they were correlated for a given dimension. The implication is that there is a general tendency for people to think of themselves as similar or different in comparison with their associates, and a tendency for the group to see various members as having much or little in common with the group, but these two aspects are not highly related.

Respondents were scored in terms of improvement or decline in mental health scores[6] on (1) semantic differential measure of self-esteem, (2) semantic differential measure of satisfaction with self, and (3) Taylor Manifest Anxiety Scale. These changes were correlated with the AS measures, giving the results shown in Table 3.19. Both AS indices show significant associations with changes in the Taylor Manifest Anxiety Scale, $\overline{AS}_s$ shows a significant relationship with self-satisfaction, and the relationship for self-esteem is not significant, although the trend was positive. Since four of the five relationships were significant, it appears that, whether they are measured subjectively or in terms of group perceptions, people who have close ties of perceived similarity to their peers are more likely to show improvement on indices of generalized subjective distress. Although the statistics and measures are rather complicated, both the fact that Fiedler's research is a true longitudinal study and the pattern of the results (but not the sizes of the associations, which are quite small) give strong support to the hypothesis suggested by Rosenberg's study.

[6]The actual statistical procedures involved a complicated control for measurement regression which need not concern us in this context.

Table 3.19 Significant Relationships between Assumed Similarity and Change in Mental Health

Measure	$\overline{AS}_g$	$\overline{AS}_s$
Taylor	*	**
Self-satisfaction	†	**
Self-esteem	†	NS

NS = Not significant.
* Significant at .05 level.
** Significant at .01 level.
† Not calculated because of technical statistical problems.

CONCLUSION 16

There is scanty but fairly persuasive research evidence that a high rate of contact within informal groups of homogeneous people facilitates mental health.

Religion.   The idea that acceptance of a religious faith has favorable consequences for mental health is part both of popular opinion (42 per cent of Nunnally's general population disagreed with the statement "People who attend church regularly are as likely to end up in a mental hospital as those who do not") and of mass-media campaigns ("The family that prays together stays together"). Unlike popular beliefs about rural, urban, and SES differences, there is some evidence to support this proposition, although not enough to suggest why it should be true—whether it is because religious people are involved in social ties in their congregation, because philosophical systems of belief provide security, because religious belief is an index of general acceptance of conventional standards, etc.

To begin with, there is no evidence that adherents of particular religions vary in their degree of mental health. The Midtown study (Srole *et al.*, 1962, p. 321) found no consistent differences among Protestants, Catholics, and Jews, although Jews did have higher rates of outpatient treatment, which can be explained by their very high acceptance of psychotherapy. *Americans View Their Mental Health* (Gurin *et al.*, 1960, pp. 238–45) shows differences between Protestants and Catholics on some items, but over the range of measures neither Protestants nor Catholics have more than their share of favorable or unfavorable scores. That is, the two Christian faiths differ somewhat in kind of mental health problem but probably not in degree. Two studies, however, show lower levels of mental health on subjective measures for the less religious (defined as infrequent church attenders) regardless of their particular major religious group.

Americans View Their Mental Health, again our best source of such data, reports tabulations separately for Catholics and Protestants by frequency of church attendance for ten measures. On the symptom indices "Martial Inadequacy," "Parental Inade-

Education for Positive Mental Health

Table 3.20 Frequency of Church Attendance, by Happiness and Role Adjustment

Measure	Religion	More than Once a Week	Once a Week	A Few Times a Month	A Few Times a Year	Never	Q (Once a Week or More v. Less Often)
Happiness (*very happy*)	Protestant	44 (193)	39 (507)	32 (446)	34 (454)	22 (139)	+.172
	Catholic	33 (98)	39 (310)	25 (64)	27 (51)	†	+.271
Marital happiness (*very happy*)	Protestant	50 (144)	51 (372)	47 (346)	37 (363)	35 (86)	+.199
	Catholic	59 (66)	51 (256)	36 (55)	33 (39)	†	+.354
Job satisfaction (*very satisfied*)*	Protestant	37 (49)	35 (135)	26 (388)		18 (60)	+.235
	Catholic	41 (27)	29 (126)	14 (51)		†	+.468

*Tabulated for men only.
†Case base too small to justify tabulations.

quacy," and "Work Problems," there is no consistent difference which holds for both Protestants and Catholics and in both sexes. However, for "Happiness," "Marital Happiness," and "Job Satisfaction," favorable percentages increase steadily with church attendance (Gurin *et al.*, 1960, Tabular Supplement, pp. B-50 – B-61). Table 3.20 gives these results. The rank orders are reasonably consistent, and the Q's suggest that religious involvement contributes to the happiness of contemporary Americans to about the same degree as education but less than money. It is perhaps worth noting that the relationships are not monotonic in a strict sense, for the group reporting attendance more than once a week is not consistently higher than the group reporting weekly attendance. This suggests that religious participation beyond the conventional weekly norm for Christians has no particular benefit to mental health, although participation below the conventional norm is associated with lowered scores.

Gurin and his colleagues do not report controls for age, education, or marital status, but the NORC survey of arts and science graduates provides a rough approximation, since the entire sample consists of young, extremely well-educated respondents, with only a handful of divorced or widowed persons. Here, too, there is a tendency for religious participation to be associated with positive scores, as can be seen in Table 3.21. The coefficients are indeed modest in size, but all except two are in a favorable direc-

Table 3.21 Q Coefficients with Frequency of Church Attendance

Index (Response Given in Parentheses)	Q
Spirits (good)	+.259
Can't force self (low)	+.202
Insomnia (low)	+.155
Blues (low)	+.144
Goal confusion (low)	+.130
School worries (low)	+.108
Good time in school (yes)	+.095
Health (favorable)	+.076
Financial worries (low)	+.061
Appetite (low)	−.040
Headaches (low)	−.006

tion, and the two exceptions are very close to zero. On the other hand, it could be argued that, compared with the general population, the graduate students are subjected to fewer pressures toward religious involvement and find more support for secular and rationalist ideologies. If so, the finding is perhaps a little more impressive than the sizes of the coefficients would otherwise warrant.

Again we can say nothing about the direction of the causal trend (although common sense would suggest that troubled people increase their rates of church attendance rather than decrease them) or the precise mechanism underlying the association, but it does appear that religious involvement is favorable to mental health. Certainly the evidence lies against the idea that the maladjusted are especially prone to involvement in religious affairs.

CONCLUSION 17
People whose rates of religious participation are below the conventional norm tend to have less favorable scores on indices of mental health, although the evidence gives no hint of the reasons.

Past Experiences and Mental Health

Although mental health education assumes that contemporary environmental pressures have a strong effect on mental health, it also assumes that past experiences have a permanent impact on the individual, so that people in the same environment will show different mental health states. The ideas are not contradictory, and their relationships can be expressed in terms of the scheme shown by the accompanying tabulation, in which, for purposes of exposition, we construct a world where there are only two kinds of environments—"favorable" and "unfavorable"—and two kinds of histories—"favorable" and "unfavorable." The tabulation shows four categories of results produced by the effects of history and environment, which may be interpreted as follows. In the first situation, "Environmental Determination," mental health varies with the environment, regardless of the individual's previous history. In the second situation, "Historical Determination," people with unfavorable histories have lower favorable histories have high mental health regardless of their circumstances. In the third situation both past histories and current environment affect mental health, which is high for those with favorable histories in favorable situations and low for those with unfavorable histories in unfavorable situations. The fourth situation produces a logically different situation, analogous to the idea of predisposition. Here neither environment nor past history contributes independently, but those people with an unfavorable history as well as an unfavorable environment have lower mental health, while the other three possible types do not differ.

Effects on Mental Health

Environmental Determination

History	Environment	
	Favorable	Unfavorable
Favorable	High	Low
Unfavorable	High	Low

Historical Determination

History	Environment	
	Favorable	Unfavorable
Favorable	High	High
Unfavorable	Low	Low

Additive

History	Environment	
	Favorable	Unfavorable
Favorable	High	Medium
Unfavorable	Medium	Low

Predisposition

History	Environment	
	Favorable	Unfavorable
Favorable	High	High
Unfavorable	High	Low

As our previous considerations of the available literature might suggest, we could find no single study which was designed so that the reactions of persons with various histories could be compared over various situations. Such a design is much more complicated than was attempted in any of the studies reviewed — and one which almost necessarily implies longitudinal research running into decades. However, this scheme does provide a framework for evaluating the scraps of evidence which are available. Of the studies collected, only Star's (1949*b*) data on the effects of combat approximate the necessary design. We showed in previous discussion of Star's work that both level of education and degree of exposure to combat influenced one's score on mental health measures. In a sense the findings fit our "Additive" situation, if one considers proximity to combat as an environmental variation and calls level of education an index of favorable history. As in our hypothetical example, adjustment scores varied from highly educated soldiers not exposed to combat at one extreme to highly uneducated soldiers involved in "actual combat" at the other extreme. Furthermore, the progression in scores was regular for each variable in each row and column, suggesting that the "Predisposition" model does not fit these data.

The only additional evidence we found comes from four studies involving continuity over time in mental health. If one is willing to assume that, over a period of time, environmental stress varies considerably, then any studies which show high correlations between mental health states over a period of time support the idea of what we have called "Historical Determination" as a factor, although they are still somewhat compatible with the "Additive" or "Predisposition" models.

As for longitudinal studies of mental health, our survey of the literature uncovered only the studies listed below.

1. Rosenberg's (1962) study of high-school students, described in the previous section, provides circumstantial evidence on continuity in mental health states. That is, since he shows an association between one's neighborhood situation during grammar school and his adjustment in the later years of high school, we must infer a continuity to mental health despite the variability in the student's current situations. The technical purist may, of

course, maintain that the maladjusted student would be more likely to misperceive his early environment as hostile, so that true continuity has not been demonstrated.

2. The *American Soldier* studies provide two isolated sets of data on test-retest scores for their mental health measures. Star (1949*b*, p. 503), in discussing the construction of the Psychosomatic Complaints Score, reports correlations of .93 and .90, respectively, for administrations of the instruments one week apart in a sample consisting of psychoneurotic patients and of enlisted men on duty. But because the environmental stress of soldiers should not be expected to vary much in a week, the finding is much less impressive substantively than it is as evidence for the technical quality of the measure. Much more impressive is a correlation over two years reported in the analysis of Stouffer and DeVinney (1949, pp. 162 – 63). They present answers on the "Good Spirits" question by 110 men measured in 1943 in the United States and again in 1945 in Europe, after combat. The point bi-serial correlation of .48 suggests substantial continuity. (For comparison with some of our other data, our calculations give a Q of .78 for the table; Q's always run considerably higher than correlations on the same data.) Since these men had been exposed to two years of army life, to movement from the United States to Europe, to combat, and apparently to the intervening event of conclusion of the European War, the degree of continuity is remarkable.

3. Kendall (1954), in her book *Conflict and Mood*, presents data on a similar "Good Spirits" item in a four-week test-retest among a sample of 513 college students enrolled in sociology departments at Northwestern University, New Jersey College for Women, Smith College, Columbia University School of General Studies, and the University of Connecticut's Department of Psychology. Our calculated Q coefficient of .29 for her question is only moderate, but in a sense it is remarkably high, since the question was worded in a way that was biased against continuity in response, as follows.

As you know from your own experience, everyone has "ups and downs" in mood. We want to know how you feel about yourself and life

Education for Positive Mental Health

in general today. We don't want you to answer in terms of how you feel "usually" or "most of the time," but how you feel today.

First of all, we would like to know whether you are in pretty good spirits or pretty bad spirits today.

Given these instructions, we may interpret a Q of .29 as supporting considerable continuity, even though the period of one month is too small to allow for much change in environmental stress.

4. The St. Louis follow-up study (O'Neal and Robins, 1958*a*, *b*), discussed above in terms of the relationships between SES and mental health, provides the longest span of coverage of any study we examined and in fact, as far as we can tell, is the only existing longitudinal study of mental health in which respondents were followed from youth to maturity.[7] Because of the strategic significance of this study, it is worthwhile to review its procedures carefully.

1. Out of a population of 2,505 referrals to the St. Louis Municipal Psychiatric Clinic in the years 1924–29, 524 cases were selected in the 1950's on the following criteria: (*a*) age under eighteen at time of referral, (*b*) IQ of 80 or higher, (*c*) Caucasian, (*d*) referred for problem behavior, not placement or vocational choice, and (*e*) existence of adequate records.
2. The authors state that the patients were "very rarely" treated by the clinic, which existed for diagnostic and referral purposes.
3. The authors selected 100 controls from the public schools and matched them by sex, race, year of birth, place of residence, and IQ. Controls were excluded if there were repetition of a grade, excessive absences, or transfer to a correctional institution.

[7] The famous long-term study of 1,500 gifted children who have been followed since 1921, done by Terman and Oden (1959), at first glance seems to be an exception. However, the analysts, in the five volumes of reports, never correlate prior characteristics with later adjustment but devote their analysis of adjustment to panegyrics on the high adjustment level of their sample, a point long ago granted. Analyses of these data in terms of prior measures predictive of later adjustment would be an extremely significant contribution to the knowledge of mental health, particularly since thirty-nine of the subjects were known to have been hospitalized for mental illness.

4. At the time of publication, 85 per cent of the total cases had been located (76 per cent of the controls and 58 per cent of the patients were still in the city), and 150 of the total of 624 cases had been interviewed.

5. Psychiatric diagnoses of current adjustment were made by three independent psychiatrists from the interview protocols, although no information is given on how the final ratings were determined.

Although a number of quibbles may be raised — the first 150 cases may not be representative; the spatial-mobility differences in the samples suggest that the patients (presumably local) who were interviewed early may not be representative; the measure of childhood mental health (referral to a clinic) technically falls out of our classification; etc. — the study is a considerable accomplishment.

The general outline of the findings reported (see Table 3.22) suggests considerable continuity of adjustment. To begin with, the contemporary adjustment of ex-patients twenty or more years later appears to be less desirable than that of controls. Furthermore, among the patients, a simple count of the total symptoms in the original record (Table 3.23) is predictive of the later diagnosis of schizophrenia. Even though the case bases are very small, the evidence is all in favor of the hypothesis that mental health states have considerable continuity. Interestingly, though, this study casts considerable doubt upon a favorite hypothesis in the field of mental health. Remembering from Chapter 2 the ways in which schoolteachers since the 1920's have come around to the belief of mental health experts that it

Table 3.22 Per Cent Rated as Low in Adjustment: Ex-patients and Controls

Controls	Patients			
	Total	Neurotic	Delinquent	Antisocial
37 (35)	76 (115)	64 (33)	80 (35)	81 (47)

Q, controls *v.* total patients, .69; Q, controls *v.* neurotics, .50.

104
Education for Positive Mental Health

is the shy, quiet child who is in need of mental health aid, it is ironic that the theme of the only longitudinal study we discovered is the finding that the aggressive, antisocial youth has a worse prognosis than the neurotic child, both in terms of adjustment ratings and later SES. If the O'Neal and Robins findings should be corroborated in other research, one of the minor tasks of mental health education in the future may be to undo one of its areas of success in the past.

CONCLUSION 18
We found no studies bearing on the relative contributions of past histories and contemporary environments to adult mental health, but the scattered evidence that mental health states are surprisingly constant over time does suggest a historical continuity to adult mental health.

CHILDREN'S EMOTIONAL DEVELOPMENT
As the assumptions of mental health education are formulated in Chapter 1, it is impossible to draw a firm line between "child development" and "mental health." Consequently, anyone attempting to review what is known about the mental health aspects of child-rearing is faced with the formidable task of reviewing all that is known about child development — an impossible assignment. We gain some selectivity by sticking narrowly to the scheme set forth at the end of Chapter 1. Thus we shall limit ourselves to two questions; first, "What is known about the practices of parents and their children's emotional development?" and second, "What is known about the mental health of parents and their children's mental health?"

Table 3.23 Follow-up Diagnosis and Original Symptoms

Total Symptoms in Original Record	Schizophrenic (Per Cent)	No Disease (Per Cent)
15 and over	25	12
10–14	39	21
1–9	36	67
Total	100	100
N	28	57

Parental Practices and Children's Emotional Development
The very fact that we are raising the question of the relationship between parental practices and children's mental health
reflects the tremendous impact of mental health education on
modern America. While no culture or historical period has been
without advice to parents on how to bring up children, the idea
that parents can affect their children's emotional adjustment by
choice of practice is a product of twentieth-century psychological
doctrines.

During this century, the content of fashionable psychological
doctrines has fluctuated wildly. During the twenties behaviorism
was in the saddle, while during the thirties and forties classical
Freudian and neo-Freudian doctrines held sway among the
experts — particularly those associated with the "culture and
personality" school in anthropology (Margaret Mead, Geoffrey
Gorer, etc.). Despite considerable hostility between proponents
of these two approaches, both assume a correlation between
specific practice and general adjustment. The behaviorist, thinking in terms of discrete stimuli and responses, reinforcement and
conditioning, was led to focus on specific aspects of child care,
such as scheduling of feeding. Despite very different assumptions, the doctrines of psychosexual development, libido, and
symbolic significance led the Freudian to focus on the physio-
logical development of the child and the parental behavior associated with it — toilet-training, breast-feeding, etc. Thus, although
their premises were different, experts' discussions of child-
rearing up to the end of World War II focused heavily on choice
of specific techniques — demand feeding versus scheduled feeding, corporal punishment, appropriate timing of toilet-training,
rooming-in, breast-feeding, enuresis. It is no accident that the
best publicized mental health education pamphlet, *Pierre the
Pelican*, deals with specific techniques of infant care.

These ideas were essentially supported by arguments from
abstract doctrine and clinical examples; the general line of "hard"
research evidence shows practically no correlation between
specific parental practice and children's adjustment. We shall
note three examples of this negative evaluation.

1. Harold Orlansky (1949) reported on a review of 149 titles

in the area of "infant care and personality." He concluded the following.

> We are led to reject the thesis that specific nursing disciplines have a specific, invariant psychological impact on the child. Instead, it appears that the effect of a particular discipline can be determined only from knowledge of the parental attitudes associated with it, the value which the culture places upon that discipline, the organic constitution of the infant, and the entire sociocultural situation in which the individual is located.

2. The definitive study in the area, published after Orlansky's review, is that of William H. Sewell (1952). His sample consists of 162 farm children, of "old American stock," aged five and six, from unbroken marriages, and apparently from a single Wisconsin community. Sewell obtained the following measures of children's adjustment.

1. California test of personality
2. Haggerty-Olson-Wickman Behavior Rating Scale (teacher-rating)
3. Wisconsin test of personality (projective)
4. General adjustment index (based on interview with mother regarding nervous symptoms and "emotional adjustment")

From personal interviews with the mother, Sewell obtained scales for seven specific child-rearing techniques: (1) breast- versus bottle-feeding, (2) self- versus demand-feeding schedule, (3) gradual versus sudden weaning, (4) late versus early bowel-training, (5) late versus early bladder-training, (6) punishment for toilet accidents versus no punishment, (7) whether child slept with mother.

For each technique, forty-six tests could be made on various scales and subscales of adjustment. Thus there were 322 possible associations (seven techniques times forty-six tests), of which 14 were significant (11 in the predicted direction and 3 in the reverse direction) and 308 were not significant. Since statistically one would expect 5 per cent of all associations to be significant at the .05 level in repeated samplings from a data matrix made up of random numbers, and the 14 associations represent 4 per cent of the 322 relationships, the conclusion drawn is that there is no association between infant training practices and the later adjustment of these children. Of course, rural Wisconsin children may be unrepresentative (but it would be difficult to deduce from theories of child-rearing why the relationships should not hold in Wisconsin rural areas) and mothers' reports may not be entirely accurate. But at the very least, the Sewell study shifts the burden of proof onto the shoulders of anyone who claims a correlation between infant-care practices and later adjustment. Since, in addition, Brim (1959, p. 44) cites several other similar studies which we did not review for our analysis, the point is not much in doubt.

CONCLUSION 19
There is no evidence for a correlation between specific infant-handling techniques and children's later adjustment.

Faced with consistently negative evidence (as rare in behavioral-science research as consistently positive evidence), the experts, except for a handful of orthodox analysts, have abandoned the assumption that one can influence a child's adjustment through choice of infant-handling techniques. Because ideas of this sort move through society fairly slowly, it will be some time before pediatricians and health educators abandon the idea, and even longer before the less educated general population (who Bronfenbrenner shows are just beginning to adopt the idea) adopt it and then abandon it.

Because experts are required in the nature of their role to have some advice to give, new doctrines must rush in to fill the void created by the collapse of "culture and personality" principles. As in its contemporary politics, America's contemporary child-development ideas lack clear-cut ideological lines, and it is hard to sort contemporary positions into clear-cut camps. In fact, rather than opposing schools of child-rearing developing, as was the case with the behaviorists and Freudians, it is our impression that what is happening is that a common acceptance of what we have called the "thermodynamic" theory is developing, in which differences among the experts reflect the route by which they reach the conclusion, rather than the conclusion itself. Such trends cannot be documented statistically, but we can note the following developments, in addition to the previous discussion of Nunnally's data and of Spock.

1. *Patterns of Child Rearing* (Sears *et al.*, 1957), although published less than a decade ago, has had considerable impact on experts' thinking. To begin with, it went a long way toward unseating the "social class and child-rearing" variant of "culture and personality" doctrines — the idea that lower-class people use permissive child-rearing techniques and their children are well-adjusted but unambitious, while middle-class people use strict techniques and their children are maladjusted but ambitious. More important, though, the authors interpret a number of their findings in a way which is congruent with the warmth theory. Illustrations (Sears *et al.*, 1957, pp. 482–83, 484, 388) are given below.

Perhaps the most pervasive quality we attempted to measure was the warmth of the mother's feeling for her child. . . . Warmth proved equally pervasive in its effects on the child. Maternal *coldness* was associated with the development of feeding problems and persistent bed-wetting. It contributed to high aggression. It was an important background condition for emotional upset during severe toilet training, and for the slowing of conscience development.

Punitiveness, in contrast with rewardingness, was quite ineffectual quality for a mother to inject into her child training. The evidence for this conclusion is overwhelming. The unhappy effects of punishment have run like a dismal thread through our findings.

The pattern most calculated to produce "high conscience" should be that of mothers who are usually warm and loving, and then, as a method of control, threaten this affectionate relationship . . . this is indeed the case.

The logical and empirical interrelations of "warmth," "punitiveness," "reward," "withdrawal of love," etc., are so complicated that they must be analyzed in some detail to be useful. For instance, it is impossible to deduce from such general ideas as "warmth is the most important aspect of child-rearing" whether a mother's withdrawal of love (defined by Sears *et al.* as "indicating to the child that her warmth and affection toward him are conditional to his good behavior") is a very useful technique or a sin against the principles of child-rearing. In order to introduce some order into these problems, Sears *et al.* (1957, p. 478) introduce two distinctions: (1) "Love-oriented" techniques (her own love and affection) versus "Object-oriented" techniques (material or physical things that the child either wants or wants to avoid); and (2) "Positive" controls (offering rewards or incentives) versus "Negative" controls (threat, punishment, deprivation of privilege). A cross-classification of these yields four basic techniques, as shown in the tabulation herewith.

While the authors do not specifically introduce the idea as part of their classification, it is clear from their analysis that they consider "warmth" something still different—a relatively permanent level of affectional demonstration which provides the background for any particular technique. The result is an eight-fold classification of situations, the application of the four techniques within the two background levels. Unfortunately, all these variables are intercorrelated—mothers who use only physical punishment tend to be classified as cold, not warm, etc. Therefore, unless data on all three variables are presented simultaneously, it is impossible to assess the results. Consequently, the isolated finding that physical punishment is ineffective can be used to support the idea that (*a*) overall warmth is more effective than coldness, (*b*) love-oriented techniques are more effective than object-oriented techniques, and (*c*) positive controls are more effective than negative controls.

In a few instances, however, Sears *et al.* (1957, pp. 125, 388, 335) present tables which enable us to make a preliminary guess.

Technique	Positive	Negative	
Love-oriented	A. Praise	B.	{ Isolation { Withdrawal of love
Object-oriented	C. Tangible rewards	D.	{ Deprivation of privileges { Physical punishment

We reproduce them as Tables 3.24, 3.25, and 3.26. There is no magic formula in these tables. Neither the type of technique nor generalized warmth has a positive effect across the board. Thus, warmth is associated with positive results for those giving severe toilet-training, for both techniques in the case of conscience, and

Table 3.24 Per Cent of Children Who Showed No Upset over Toilet-training

Classification of Mother	Technique*	
	Mild (A, C, and None)	Severe (B, D)
Warm	79 (112)	77 (48)
Cold	89 (101)	52 (98)

*Severity rated on the degree of scolding, disapproval, anger, punishment, etc.

Table 3.25 Percentage of Children with High Conscience*

Classification of Mother	Technique (Withdrawal of Love)	
	Little or None (A, C, D)	Fairly Often (B)
Warm	24	42
Cold	18	25

*N's not reported.

Table 3.26 Percentage of Mothers Who Reported That Spanking Did Their Children Good

Classification of Mother	Technique (Physical Punishment)	
	Infrequent (A, B, C)	Frequent (D)
Warm	42 (101)	66 (65)
Cold	41 (98)	43 (111)

for frequent spankers. But for infrequent spankers warmth makes no difference, and for mild toilet-trainers warmth makes for slightly more frequent upsets. What might be said is that warmth affects the outcome by making the other techniques more effective. In the cases of conscience and spanking, it is clear that the technique is more effective among warm mothers, and in the case of toilet-training, the "bad" technique is less "bad" among warm mothers.

There is no reason to believe that these three tables are representative of all the data in the study. In fact, it is safe to say that an author is more likely to print the full table when a variable has a complicated relationship than when it has a simple relationship, and a table is even less likely to appear when the variable has no relationship. Nor is it clear that these three items necessarily tap mental health variables of the sort we have been discussing. At the same time, this influential study is the only source on the effectiveness of warmth that we discovered.

CONCLUSION 20

The only study we could find bearing on maternal warmth tentatively suggests that it operates not as an independent factor but as a factor making other psychological techniques of child-rearing more effective.

CONCLUSION 21

The only study found on the effectiveness of psychological techniques (as opposed to techniques of infant care) suggests that such techniques are effective, but their effectiveness varies with the specific situation and the mother's warmth.

2. A second route to the "warmth" theory of child-rearing has been through an influential monograph by a British psychiatrist, *Maternal Care and Mental Health* (Bowlby, 1951). Bowlby reviews a large number of clinical studies of orphans, institutionalized children, children evacuated during World War II, and so on, with the following conclusion (p. 46).

It is submitted that the evidence is now such that it leaves no room for doubt regarding the general proposition—that the prolonged deprivation of the young child from maternal care may [*sic*] have grave and far reaching effects on his character and on the whole of his future life.

Bowlby's work has received considerable attention and has gained very wide acceptance. *Mental Health Education: A Critique* (Pennsylvania Mental Health, Inc., 1960, p. 26) for example, reports the following.

A certain number of fledgling principles of mental health came up for intensive discussion. . . . Probably the most widely accepted was the thesis put forward by John Bowlby . . . that very young infants exposed to frequent changes of "mother" figures have an exceedingly poor prognosis for subsequent mental health.

Just as the research of Sears and his collaborators reflects psychological learning theory as an approach to the problem and statistical analyses as a technique of research, Bowlby's work stems from a psychiatric theoretical approach and the tradition of clinical research. But both influential studies can be interpreted as stressing the crucial importance for warm maternal contacts with the child. It is particularly interesting to view both studies in terms of an intellectual shift from the recent past, when considerable attention was given to the presumed negative consequences of "maternal overprotection" and "schizophrenic mothers," and "Mom" was a target of opprobrium for popular authors. Clearly, Mom is back in fashion.

Unfortunately, Bowlby's writings have induced considerable methodological controversy. There is very little doubt that the institutionalized and orphaned children in his studies show lower levels of development and mental health. What have been subject to considerable doubt are the implications that these deficits are permanent and that they are due to maternal deprivation. None of the studies Bowlby cities employs sufficient controls or follows its cases long enough to meet these technical objections. In an extended battle, which we need not review in detail, Bowlby's work and that of R. A. Spitz, who has put forth a very similar proposition, have been subject to rather fierce criticism by academic psychologists and have been equally fiercely defended by psychiatrists and clinicians.

Within the confines of the rules laid down for our search of the literature (general population samples, appropriate designs, appropriate statistical procedures), no studies we saw directly confirmed or negated the Bowlby hypothesis, although we can cite some indirect evidence in the following section.

CONCLUSION 22
The evidence for and against the proposition that maternal deprivation is a causative factor in poor mental health is not sufficient to justify a conclusion.

Parental Mental Health and Children's Mental Health

The final assumption of mental health education we will review is that children's mental health is affected by parental mental health and thus that mental health states have a continuity over a period of time. As with many of the ideas we have reviewed, the precise mechanism is not spelled out. It is not clear whether poorly adjusted parents have a directly harmful influence on their children, whether they choose the wrong techniques of child-rearing, or whether they lack the warmth which is believed to be a favorable condition. Furthermore, such a hypothesis always presents a knotty methodological problem, in that similarity between the mental health of parents and children may merely reflect a common third factor (heredity, common SES, common environment), rather than a causal relationship. We shall be able to present fairly consistent evidence on the correlation but very little knowledge about the mechanism which explains it.

Actually, only one study provides direct data (MacFarlane, 1943; MacFarlane *et al.*, 1954), but it is an excellent study. In the California Guidance Study, every third child born in Berkeley, California, between January 1 and June 30, 1929, was followed to age fourteen by means of annual interviews and tests. The initial sample consisted of 126 controls and 126 experimental cases who received special counseling. For reasons unknown to us, very few of the potentially very important findings of this study have been published, but luckily the question of correlates of children's and parents' adjustment is treated in a summary article (MacFarlane, 1943). The dependent variables consist of mothers' reports on twelve frequent adjustment problems of their children during ages twenty-one to thirty-six months. As we would expect from our review of adult data on age, there is a distinct SES difference, but MacFarlane (1943, pp. 322, 323) writes the following.

Among the 12 most frequent problems at these early years, in only 1, *viz.*, specific fears, were correlations with low economic status as high as those with straining interpersonal family relationships, although lower economic levels furnished more problem recruits than did higher levels.

Marital adjustment yielded more consistent and higher correlations with behavior and personality difficulties than did other family variables. Attention demanding, temper tantrums, negativism, food finickiness, overdependence, and daytime enuresis showed more recruits from families with unhappy or difficult marital adjustment. With increasing age, tempers and negativism showed increasing relationships with marital adjustment during this early preschool period. Thumb sucking and nocturnal enuresis, on the other hand, showed more recruits from happy and mutually supporting marital relationships.

The usual problems are here: marital adjustment, as we have seen, is only one aspect of adult mental health; two of the measures of children's adjustment show opposite trends; it is not impossible that the children's problems exacerbated the marital tensions; and so on, but the hypothesized correlation is demonstrated.

The remaining studies provide a consistent but less direct support for the same idea. They are studies showing a correlation between later mental health and reported family situations during childhood. More specifically, they concern information about whether the family was unbroken, broken by death, or broken by divorce or separation. The classification by parental status appears extremely crude at first glance, but further consideration suggests that it contains some interesting facets. To begin with, we shall assume on the basis of material reviewed above that divorce indicates, if not generally unfavorable mental health (which the findings of Gurin *et al.* [1960] suggest) at least unfavorable states in the marital-happiness component of mental health. On the other hand, we can assume that death is a random variable unrelated to the parents' adjustment. If so, then some interesting possibilities turn up.

1. To the extent that children from families broken by death *or* divorce show lower mental health, we have support for the idea that family disruption of the type analyzed by Bowlby has a negative effect on children's mental health.
2. To the extent that children from families broken by divorce show lower mental health than those from families broken by death, we have support for the idea that parental adjustment contributes to lowered mental health beyond the impact of family disruptions.

A complete analysis would require controls for the sex of the parent and the age at which disruption occurred, but we found no such data, so we can only compare the three situations. Even so, the results are fairly consistent.

1. Although the case base is very small, O'Neal and Robins (1958*b*) report such data from their follow-up study of guidance-clinic cases and controls. Table 3.27 summarizes their results. Within the two groups taken together, there is no difference between the "Not Broken" and the "Death" groups, and there are insufficient cases among the controls to examine the effects of divorce and separation. However, when we separately examine the results within each of these two groups, we are, in effect, holding constant the level of adjustment during childhood. When we examine the total (remembering that the exact percent-

Table 3.27 Per Cent Rated Other than "Well Adjusted" in Follow-up Home Situation before Eighteenth Birthday

Group	Not Broken	Death	Divorce or Separation
Experimentals	82 (50)	70 (30)	86 (35)
Controls	31 (26)	38 (8)	* (1)
Total	68 (76)	63 (38)	83 (36)

*Too small to percentage.

age is artificial, because controls are not present in their true proportion in the population, we see a high rate of impairment for children of divorced parents—a relationship otherwise concealed because all but one of the children of divorced parents were in the experimental (less well-adjusted) group to begin with. The suggestion of these tentative findings is that divorce, but not death, is associated with lower mental health.

2. The *American Soldier* studies provide additional, but quite guarded, corroboration for these differences. Stouffer and DeVinney (1949, pp. 132–34) compare answers to the question, "Did your parents always live together up to the time you were sixteen years old?" for a cross-section of enlisted men, a group of "best-adjusted soldiers" (who gave favorable answers to several morale and esprit items of the type discussed previously) and hospitalized neurotic soldiers. Their results are given in Table 3.28. Because of the large sample, the differences are statistically significant. The hospitalized neurotic soldiers do prove to be more likely to come from broken homes, but the differences are quite small. That is, if divorce or death of a parent raises one's probability of maladjustment, but only 2 or 3 per cent, it certainly cannot be considered a major factor in adult adjustment. Furthermore, Stouffer notes (and his finding is con-

Table 3.28 Comparisons of Home Situation for a Cross-Section of Enlisted Men, a Group of "Best-adjusted Soldiers," and Hospitalized Neurotic Soldiers

"Did your parents always live together up to the time you were 16 years old?"	Best-adjusted Soldiers (Per Cent)		Cross-Section (Per Cent)		Hospitalized Neurotic Soldiers (Per Cent)		Q (Neurotic v. Cross-Section)
Yes	76		77		70		−.178
No	21		21		27		
Death		14		15		17	+.074
Divorce or separation		7		6		10	+.270
No answer	3		2		2		
Total	100		100		99		
N	410		3,729		613		

sistent with a wide variety of studies of SES) that there is a considerable association between education and broken homes, family disruption being more frequent among those with less education. If SES were introduced as a control, it is possible that these small differences would vanish.

3. Gurin *et al.* (1960, p. 246) similarly compared the answers of those from intact families, homes broken through death, and homes broken through divorce. Their conclusions are as follows.

On the indices of general adjustment, there are surprisingly few differences among the three groups. In particular, growing up in a home disorganized by the death of a parent does not seem to have any special bearing on the experiences of general adjustment. People who were raised in homes in which parents were divorced or separated, however, are distinctive in some respects.

Our calculation of Q coefficients from the percentages they report, shown in Table 3.29, provides detail to supplement their general statement. Although the coefficients are smaller than many we have considered, the children of divorced parents do show a consistently less favorable pattern, while the children of families suffering the death of a parent are not different from the remainder of the sample.

Table 3.29 Coefficients for Family Situations and Indices of General Adjustment

Measure	Death of Parent v. Intact*	Divorce or Separation v. Intact
Happiness	−.07	−.16
Marital happiness	−.06	−.14
Marital inadequacy	−.05	−.34
Marriage problems	.00	−.38
Psychological anxiety	−.10	−.12
Physical health	+.03	−.05
Immobilization	+.05	−.21
Physical anxiety	+.08	−.18

Source: Gurin et al. (1960, Tabular Supplement, pp. B-63 – B-66).
* − indicates unfavorable direction.

The three studies reviewed show considerable agreement. Each leads to the idea that the death of a parent has little measurable impact on mental health, while divorce is associated with small but consistent lessening of mental health later in life. None of the three studies, however, presents data with SES controlled, and because SES is a major correlate of both family disorganization and mental health, we cannot rule out the possibility that the correlation is spurious.

CONCLUSION 23

The idea that parental mental health correlates with children's mental health is supported by the one direct study we found and by three studies which show low but consistent differences for children growing up in homes broken by divorce. But the mechanism involved is not known, and the results for divorced parents could be a spurious function of SES.

CONCLUSION 24

To the extent that death of a parent indicates maternal deprivation,[8] the studies reviewed do not support the claim that such deprivation is associated with permanent lowering of mental health.

RECOMMENDATIONS AND CONCLUSIONS

As in Chapter 2, we will not recapitulate the conclusions in detail, but for the convenience of the reader, we repeat the conclusions consecutively at the end of the discussion. But in contrast to Chapter 2, we have not, in this chapter, set forth recommendations in the various subsections. The reason is patent: in each case but one the conclusion is that further research on the topic is necessary. The exception is the cases of SES; it is clear that no further studies need be made to document the claim that

[8] As is obvious from known mortality trends, the majority of the cases coded "Death of Parent" involve the death of a father instead of a mother and thus do not really test the idea of maternal deprivation. Furthermore, we can predict that deprivation during adolescence would have an effect different from that produced by deprivation during early life. At the same time, we must assume that people who were subject to loss of a mother during early life also fall within the "Death of Parent" category, and, unless we assume that death of a father has a positive effect on mental health, they should bring down the level of the group as a whole. Either this last group is very small or the hypothesized effects are not very strong. Either interpretation casts considerable doubt on the idea that the effects of maternal deprivation provide a key to needed programs in mental health.

lower SES is associated with lower mental health. However, there is still an urgent need for studies which can explain the reasons why the well-documented SES differences exist.

That we pick and choose among the needed research smacks of arrogance, for the need actually is for broad and rapid advances across the entire spectrum of the behavioral sciences, from small-group studies (the role of peer solidarity in mental health) to child development (the effectiveness of parental techniques) to prospects of social reform (the demonstrably lower mental health of the "have-nots").

If we were to argue, however, for a single piece of research which would provide information for health educators, it would be for a large-scale longitudinal study of the mental health of school-age children. The argument stems from the fact that *Americans View Their Mental Health* and *Mental Health in the Metropolis* (both of which will continue in their analyses), as well as *The American Soldier*, have provided us with good descriptions of the adjustment of the adult general population. Certainly, numerous smaller-scale researches will be needed to fill in the gaps and to follow leads provided by these studies, but, as we have seen, these three do a good job of blocking out a previously unknown area. When we turn to studies of children and of parental behavior, however, the information thins out considerably. There have been an enormous number of studies of parents and children, of course, but they have used such small and unrepresentative samples and have been devoted to so few variables that it has been practically impossible to use them for hammering out a basic description in the way that the three studies noted above yielded a basic description of adult adjustment. It is ironic that, despite the tremendous concern for children, child-rearing, and children's mental health in modern America, there has been no study of children and parents using a national cross-section since the work of Anderson (1936). We are thus tempted to recommend what would in effect be a national replication of the study by Sears *et al.* (1957).

It is our inclination, however, to suggest that even greater rewards would come from a large-scale study of children themselves, rather than of parents and their reports of children's behavior. Because the costs of observing a large national sample of small children would be very high (the field costs alone for observing 5,000 children for one day might run to $125,000), we feel that a study of school-age children based on self-administered questionnaires would be more efficient, particularly since the evidence is against the idea that the effect of early infant-care techniques is crucial. Thus to arrange for a national probability sample of, say, 10,000 school children to fill out a yearly measure of their mental health status and information on their families, friends, and communities would be *relatively* easy, because data collection could be done through school systems. A genuine longitudinal study, in which the same children were measured for a period of perhaps five years, could provide a tremendous amount of information on the importance of family factors, SES, friends, and school factors. It would also provide developmental "norms" on a sample which can be generalized to the total United States population (about 98 per cent of America's children up to the age of fifteen are now enrolled in school) as well as the power in interpreting data given by longitudinal studies. Thus, for example, in a sample of 10,000 cases followed for five years we could expect that enough cases would turn up for a researcher to compare a student's mental health before and after a divorce or parental death in the family.

It is certainly not the task of Pennsylvania Mental Health, Inc.—an action agency—to conduct such a study merely because it lacks sufficient research information to plan its mental health education programs. But we recommend that, since action programs will be severely handicapped by the lack of needed basic research, Pennsylvania Mental Health might seriously consider using its good offices to urge commissioning studies of this or other kinds necessary to provide sufficient research evidence to support action programs.

The following review of the conclusions of this chapter assesses the current state of our knowledge concerning the relationships between mental health variables.

CONCLUSION 11
To the extent that there is a sex difference in mental health, women's adjustment is less favorable, but the relationship is limited to older

and less well-educated groups, and expert ratings of impairment show difference.

CONCLUSION 12

Numerous studies and findings suggest that adult mental health is more favorable in higher socio-economic status groups. However, higher education apparently produces an increased sensitivity and self-critical capacity, which slightly offsets this trend. Also, the available evidence does not enable us to determine how much of this reflects differential environmental pressures, how much reflects a superior adjustment capacity of higher-educated groups, or the extent to which SES is determined by mental health.

CONCLUSION 13

Age differences in mental health are complex, although studies tend to show less favorable results for older people. We note two contradictory trends: (1) older people are more often under environmental stresses which increase generalized subjective distress (low SES, physical illness, social isolation); and (2) older people apparently are more likely to have a "frame of reference" which softens the negative impact of environmental stresses.

CONCLUSION 14

Community differences in size and urbanization are relatively unimportant to generalized subjective distress.

CONCLUSION 15

The evidence on marital status and mental health is inconsistent, although more often than not it suggests superior adjustment for the married person.

CONCLUSION 16

There is scanty but fairly persuasive research evidence that a high rate of contact within informal groups of homogeneous people facilitates mental health.

CONCLUSION 17

People whose rates of religious participation are below the conventional norm tend to have less favorable scores on indices of mental health, although the evidence gives no hint of the reasons.

CONCLUSION 18

We found no studies bearing on the relative contributions of past histories and contemporary environments to adult mental health, but the scattered evidence that mental health states are surprisingly constant over time does suggest a historical continuity to adult mental health.

Conclusion 19

There is no evidence for a correlation between specific infant-handling techniques and children's later adjustment.

Conclusion 20

The only study we could find bearing on maternal warmth tentatively suggests that it operates not as an independent factor but as a factor making other psychological techniques of child-rearing more effective.

Conclusion 21

The only study found on the effectiveness of psychological techniques (as opposed to techniques of infant care) suggests that such techniques are effective, but their effectiveness varies with the specific situation and the mother's warmth.

Conclusion 22

The evidence for and against the proposition that maternal deprivation is a causative factor in poor mental health is not sufficient to justify a conclusion.

Conclusion 23

The idea that parental mental health correlates with children's mental health is supported by the one direct study we found and by three studies which show low but consistent differences for children growing up in homes broken by divorce. But the mechanism involved is not known, and the results for divorced parents could be a spurious function of SES.

Conclusion 24

To the extent that death of a parent indicates maternal deprivation, the studies reviewed do not support the claim that such deprivation is associated with permanent lowering of mental health.

4

Existing Knowledge: Experimental Attempts at Influence

The field studies reviewed in Chapters 2 and 3 provided a wealth of facts about the distribution of mental health variables in the American population and yielded a number of clues regarding their underlying causes. Nevertheless, such studies lack the crisp persuasive power of a well-controlled experimental study, in which the existence of carefully equated control and experimental groups adds tremendously to the validity of the conclusions.

In this chapter we review the findings from the experimental literature relevant to mental health education, considering each study as a laboratory prototype of a possible mental health education program.

None of this is to say that experiments are "better" than field studies. Indeed, we will find it harder to draw consistent conclusions in this chapter than in the analyses of preceding chapters. Most of the studies reviewed are quite deficient in sampling, many have such small case bases that negative results are almost inevitable, and in the majority of instances it is very difficult to state what the "experimental treatment" really is. Because, in addition, many of the variables which are most important for mental health are not conducive to experimental variation (poverty, marital status, combat, etc.), we must remember that both types of research have contributions to make.

Our limited search of the literature revealed forty experiments in which the dependent variable was a mental health state of the type we have considered in this volume.[1] The Annotated Bibliography evaluates these studies according to a topical outline; hence, we do not review the details of specific studies here but consider general conclusions to be drawn from the total pool of results. The following guide explains our procedure for annotation. First, studies with multiple dependent variables and/or multiple independent variables are treated as if each variable were a separate study. Second, each reference is annotated according to the following outline.

Population: The general "type" of person involved in the study (e.g., "high-school students" or "low-income mothers").

Treatment: The general class of independent variable being studied (e.g., "lecture-discussion group" or "newspaper articles").

Dependent variables: The general class or specific measure of the "effect" (e.g., "Taylor Manifest Anxiety Scale" or "attitudes toward mental patients").

Treatment groups: The manner in which experimental and control groups were made up from the population and the timing of measurements.

Results: Statistically significant differences between experimentals and controls.

Deficiencies: While we make no attempt to provide a complete methodological critique of each study, we do provide brief comments on studies with design problems that we thought were grave enough to affect interpretation. "None" should be interpreted as "no major obvious deficiencies," not as "perfection."

Over all: Classification of independent and dependent variables according to categories explained below, with outcome classified as follows: +, results suggest a demonstrable effect on the dependent variable; −, results suggest no effect on

---

[1] Although there are a large number of studies in which the *independent* variable is a mental health state (e.g., studies of the effect of anxiety on learning) these have been ignored.

dependent variable or effect opposite of that intended; *?*, results neither positive nor negative (e.g., trend in predicted direction but not statistically significant).

The existence of forty separate experiments (many more than we had anticipated when this project began) raised hopes that definite patterns of findings could be established by putting together the results from a number of experiments. Unfortunately the studies cover such a wide range of populations (from college students to low-income Negro families), treatments (from discussions led by a psychiatrist to reading the comic strip "Rex Morgan, M.D."), and dependent variables (from Taylor Manifest Anxiety score to rating mental patients "valuable or worthless") that it is seldom possible to confront pairs of studies which have more than a few aspects in common. For every contradiction in the findings, too many explanations — not too few — are suggested.

In order to introduce some organization, we have classified the independent and dependent variables in each experiment in the following manner. Dependent variables — the mental health phenomena being affected — were classified as (1) subjective states — happiness, worries, self-rating adjustment scales, etc.; (2) practices — what the respondent actually does, rather than what he says or feels (e.g., whether a mother does or does not breast-feed her child); and (3) attitudes and beliefs — whether the respondent accepts or rejects certain factual statements or certain pro-and-con positions. The classification stems from our previous chapters and is reasonably straightforward. It would be desirable to separate attitudes from beliefs, but the lack of details given by the authors in their reports and the frequent ambiguity of the distinction (is agreement with "Psychologists need to be a bit mentally unbalanced themselves in order to work with their patients" a belief or an attitude?) made such a separation impractical.

Since the lack of existing information on the factors affecting mental health states is so serious, any classification of the independent or causal variables must be a shot in the dark. Rather than follow any etiological orientation, we classified the independent variables in terms of their format, as follows: (1) media —

written or sound messages in which each subject receives the same content and there is no social interaction (give and take) between communicator and audience (e.g., pamphlets, movies, books); (2) courses — multiple sessions with a leader or instructor present and with reading or lectures, content determined by leader but some "student participation"; (3) interaction techniques — single or multiple sessions with high rates of participation by subjects and little formal presentation by leader or teacher (e.g., non-directive group therapy or role-playing sessions); and (4) miscellaneous.

The distinctions are obviously somewhat arbitrary, and perhaps the categories may best be thought of as points on a continuum from 100 per cent predetermined symbolic content (pure media) to 100 per cent spontaneous social interaction (role-playing), with most studies falling near the middle, where both media and social interaction are present (e.g., a movie followed by a group discussion). With these distinctions in mind, let us examine the patterns which emerge when we consider our studies in terms of dependent variables.

STUDIES OF ATTITUDES AND BELIEFS

Twenty-three of the forty experiments involved attitudes and beliefs as a dependent variable, and taken together they build a case for asserting that the general population is susceptible to considerable influence. Many of the studies do report failures, but the trend is positive (see Table 4.1). Of the total, thirteen report favorable results, six report negative results, and four are indeterminate. Given the vagaries of academic publications, it

Table 4.1 Outcome of Experiments Involving Attitudes and Beliefs

Outcome	Number
+	13
?	4
−	6
Total	23

would be absurd to deny that an enormous number of negative results are unpublished. Nevertheless, we can cite a variety of positive results. The following capsule summaries provide an overview of the studies with positive outcomes. Numbers after year citations are the numbers assigned to studies within volumes listed in the Annotated Bibliography.

Andrew (1954): Adult participants in a two-day mental health workshop showed improvement in information on mental health topics and in choosing appropriate reactions to hypothetical situations.

Balser *et al.* (1957), 1: Adult participants in a lecture-discussion series increased in measures of "liberalism in parent-child relations."

Ford and Hartman (1954): Mothers of small children increased in knowledge of emotional growth and development after being given a pamphlet.

McGinnies *et al.* (1958): Adults who viewed a series of three mental health films (but not those viewing just one) improved in scores on an item battery regarding mental health topics.

Nunnally (1961), 1: High-school students became more favorable toward mental patients and mental hospitals after reading one-paragraph messages on cures for mental illness.

Nunnally (1961), 2: Replication of preceding listing, with similar results.

Nunnally (1961), 3: Undergraduates became less favorable toward mental patients and treatment after receiving brief written messages first giving an explanation of mental illness and then refuting it.

Nunnally (1961), 4: High-school students learned content of brief written messages regarding mental health topics.

Nunnally (1961), 7: After exposure to false information on causes of schizophrenia, college students assimilated the information and became more favorable in attitudes toward mental patients.

Ojemann (1960): Grade-school students improved in choices of appropriate response in human-relations situations after one-year experimental course.

Owings (1931), 1: Woman improved in knowledge of sexual

information after home visit in experimental sex-education program.

Rose (1958): High-school students who read the comic strip "Rex Morgan, M.D." improved in knowledge of mental illness after reading an episode about treatment of paranoia.

Schaus (1932): Mothers who attended a course in child development improved in information about the topic.

The negative results are as follows.

Balser *et al.* (1955), 1: Two groups of teachers and administrators showed no increase in knowledge despite a fifteen-session course.

Cumming and Cumming (1957): A Canadian community showed no change in two attitude scales despite a six-month intensive mental health education campaign.

Greenberg *et al.* (1953), 1: A large sample of North Carolina mothers showed no changes in beliefs regarding infant care after receiving *Pierre the Pelican* pamphlets.

McGinnies *et al.* (1958), 2: Groups of parents viewed mental health movies, which were effective, but discussions of the movies showed no additional effect.

Nunnally (1961), 5: High-school students exposed to information about mental illness increased in information but showed variable changes in attitudes toward the mentally ill and their treatment.

Owings (1930), 3: Minneapolis mothers who received home visits regarding sex education showed an increase in information but no change in attitude.

We had little luck in finding factors which account for the differences between the successful and unsuccessful experiments. To begin with, the more sophisticated interaction techniques do not appear to be more effective than conventional forms of communication. When the attitude and belief studies are classified by format and outcome, we get the results shown in Table 4.2. The courses appear most successful and the interaction techniques the least successful, if the reported experiments are representative. Although the numbers are very small, the point is rather suggestive: a number of important studies of political campaigns have led social psychologists in recent years to doubt that mass media can switch voting intentions and to stress the importance of interpersonal relationships as an influence. While these generalizations may be quite applicable to political behavior, they have led many to discount the *general* importance of media and perhaps overstress the *general* importance of social interaction. The data in Table 4.2 suggest that the classical, unimaginative techniques of communication are just as effective as more sophisticated (and much more expensive) interaction techniques. Possibly the differences lie in the fact that in mental health communication one is more often filling a void than attempting to achieve the reversal of a strongly held belief or attitude.

Even such an obvious principle as that of "dosage" receives contradictory verdicts here. The higher success rates of the courses suggest that sheer intensity of exposure may be important. This indeed is the direct implication of the McGinnies (1958) study, which showed that viewing one mental hygiene movie did not affect attitudes, while seeing three had a significant effect. Though the Cummings (1957) fairly inundated their Canadian community with information, they observed no changes, while a number of Nunnally's (1961) experiments (subentries 2 and 6 in the Annotated Bibliography) showed significant and long-lasting effects from the reading of a single paragraph.

But content is probably more important than the communication form in determining whether a mental health education cam-

Table 4.2 Attitude and Belief Studies, by Format and Outcome

Format	Outcome		
	+	?	−
Course	4	0	1
Media	8	2	3
Interaction	0	2	1
Miscellaneous	1	0	1

paign will be successful. Because so many of the experiments treat scores on omnibus inventories which cover a wide variety of content, it is difficult to sort the studies by success and failure in specific content areas. It is perhaps more useful simply to give Nunnally's conclusions from his carefully planned program of experimental studies. Nunnally limits his research to one question—the relationship between exposure to information and changes in favorable attitudes toward mental patients and mental illness treatments—but his conclusions appear to have general importance (Nunnally, 1961, pp. 218, 220, 223, 164, 165).

Proposition 17.1: It is relatively easy to transmit mental health information effectively.

Proposition 17.2: It is more difficult to change attitudes toward mental health concepts than to increase knowledge of mental health phenomena.

Proposition 17.4: Favorable attitudes toward mental health concepts develop when people think they know something about the phenomena, regardless of whether or not their information is actually correct.

Proposition 12.1: The more certainty with which mental health information is stated, the more favorable will be the attitudes toward concepts related to the message.

Proposition 12.2: The destruction of information about mental illness without supplying new information results in negative attitudes toward related concepts.

Or, in blunter words, again Nunnally's (1961, p. 166):

The . . . results . . . demonstrate the bad effects that are obtained from communicating in an unsure, hesitant manner, and the even worse effects that are obtained by telling people only what does *not* cause mental disorder and what does *not* cure mental disorder.

What our findings indicate is that the public is not emotionally invested in its opinions about mental health to the point where it resists new ideas. Instead the public is apparently hungry for more and better information and will gobble it up when presented. Consequently, diverse methods of communication and presenting material may all be successful in improving public understanding. (What is needed is for the experts to derive a more solid body of facts to communicate to the public.)

We see no reason why Nunnally's conclusions do not apply to the acceptance of techniques of mental hygiene and prevention, as well as attitudes toward mental patients. If so, our general conclusion on attitude and belief studies is as follows.

CONCLUSION 25
The important problem, in mental hygiene campaigns concerned with techniques of personal adjustment and prevention of mental illness, is not the appropriate means of communication and persuasion but the fact that mental health educators have nothing concrete and practical to tell the public.

STUDIES OF SUBJECTIVE STATES AND PRACTICES

In the context of our project, studies of information and attitudes treat only a means to an end. More important are the thirteen studies which bear directly on the subjective states we have defined as mental health. In terms of outcome, they are distributed as shown in Table 4.3. In contrast to belief and attitude studies, negative results predominate, but there are four studies with positive results. This quartet is, from a certain point of view, the empirical rock upon which the edifice of mental health education must rest. The successful studies are the following.

Asch (1951), 2: College students in a non-directive section of a psychology course improved in MMPI adjustment scores during the semester.

Table 4.3 Outcomes of Experiments regarding Subjective States

Outcome	N
+	4
?	2
−	7

Balser *et al.* (1957), 2: Adult participants in lecture-discussion groups showed improvement on some — but not all — measures of adjustment.

Bruce (1958): Grade-school students exposed to a year's program in "causal learning" improved on adjustment scales.

Prugh *et al.* (1953): Children in an experimental ward of a children's hospital showed fewer severe reactions (crying, nightmares, etc.) than those in a control ward.

The indeterminate results are the following.

Fiedler (1949): Undergraduates anxious about exams showed a positive trend after non-directive group therapy, but the small number of cases and lack of control for grades made the experimental-control contrast statistically insignificant.

Wilner *et al.* (1962): Low-income Negro families who moved into public housing showed slightly favorable but not consistently significant advantages on self-rating adjustment scales.

The negative results are as follows.

Balser *et al.* (1955), 2: Teachers participating in a lecture-discussion series showed no improvement in adjustment.

Berkowitz (1962): Experiments on "catharsis" suggest that expression of hostility does not lower the probability of further aggression.

Leton (1957), 1: Bullis Human Relations Classes (a didactic mental health program for school children) had no significant effect on grade-school pupils' adjustment.

Leton (1957), 2: Mental hygiene movies had no significant effect on grade-school pupils' adjustment.

Leton (1957), 3: Sociodrama and role-playing had no significant effect on grade-school pupils' adjustment.

Leton (1957), 4: Hobby and crafts groups had no significant effect on grade-school pupils' adjustment.

Rogers (1960): Operant conditioning (saying "uh huh") influenced students' rates of verbalizing positive self-descriptions but not their self-rated adjustment.

The smaller number of studies and the great diversity of techniques make it even harder to find thematic generalizations in this set. Thus: (1) the two studies of lecture-discussion groups (by the same authors) show contradictory findings; (2) the two studies of school mental hygiene programs showed positive results for one (the Ojemann program) and negative results for the Bullis course, mental hygiene movies, and sociodrama; and (3) the three studies of interaction techniques show positive results for a college psychology class, indeterminate results for a nondirective college student counseling group, and negative results for role-playing among school children.

The results are too scattered to allow generalizations about promising and doubtful avenues for future research. The following comments are about all that we can make.

First, the existence of some positive results in reasonably well-controlled studies should be construed as a hopeful sign. Those who believe that adjustment is not modifiable except by lengthy psychotherapy or manipulation of environment must grant that some of the results are favorable. In fact, the statistical evidence for the efficacy of these mental health projects compares favorably with the statistical evidence for the efficacy of psychotherapy.

Second, it appears that, in comparison with information and attitude-change campaigns, programs attempting to influence subjective states must expect smaller and less decisive effects. It is not by any means impossible to influence people's adjustment (the percentage differences in the children's-hospital study are striking), but it is a very difficult task, because so many factors other than the program are operating. In particular, the clear-cut evidence that reality factors (poverty, health, family crises) play an important part in affecting subjective distress means that much of the variance in subjective distress comes from factors which cannot be changed by "educational techniques." That is, one might hope to change totally a person's beliefs about mental illness, but it is unrealistic to expect that the wife of an unemployed man can be converted from unhappy to happy, even though her adjustment might be improved through education.

It follows from these considerations that the research need is for a sheer quantitative increase in evaluation studies. It is a statistical principle that the smaller the difference becomes, the greater grows the number of observations necessary to provide reliable evidence. Thus, in election polling, much larger samples are needed to predict the winner when the final vote is 52 versus 48 per cent than when it is 75 versus 25 per cent. As it is with individual observations, so it is with studies. Since we should expect programs designed to influence adjustment to show only small effects, a large number of studies based on large numbers of subjects will be necessary before reliable conclusions can be drawn.

CONCLUSION 26
The small number of studies concerning changes in subjective states show both positive and negative results, and there are no clear-cut patterns from which to draw generalizations.

CONCLUSION 27
We can expect that even "good" programs will show relatively small effects, so it is necessary to multiply the number of evaluations and the number of cases per evaluation considerably before any general conclusions can be drawn.

Third, it is interesting that only one of the studies we reviewed concerns the most common technique of mental health education — mass media. In that study (Leton *et al.*, 1957, subentry 2 in Annotated Bibliography) it was demonstrated that grade-school students exposed to mental hygiene movies showed no change in their adjustment. The result is not encouraging, but it is hardly a fair test of the extensive labor that has been put into the preparation and distribution of books, pamphlets, comic books, magazine articles, movies, filmstrips, and so on. While it may be obvious to the sophisticated that this deluge of print and sound is useless, behavioral-science researchers have long ago learned that documenting the obvious is not always possible. In particular, the positive results from information and attitude studies such as Nunnally's warn us not to write off these techniques without a fair test.

There is an additional argument for further testing here: the argument of practicality. Given (*a*) the high cost of treatment by professional psychologists and psychiatrists; (*b*) the limited size of a discussion group or class; and (c) the known biases in volunteers for mental health programs (young, highly educated women — the people who need it least — predominate), compared with the low cost, limitless capacity, and relatively greater penetration of media techniques, we may argue that mass media are "more efficient" in the following sense. Let us assume that 10 per cent of the people exposed to an intensive program such as a lecture-discussion course show some change, while only 1 per cent of those exposed to a pamphlet show a change. If, however, the cost of reaching a person with a pamphlet is less than one-tenth of that for an intensive technique, the same amount of money invested in pamphlets will produce a greater effect than investing it in a "more effective" intensive program.

One may doubt that exposure to a mental health pamphlet will result in striking changes for a large proportion of the readers, but if one is satisfied with small changes among a large absolute number of readers, mass-media techniques deserve a fair trial.

The nub of the problem is that it is not known whether these materials have any effects at all. A design for such a study is proposed in Chapter 5.

CONCLUSION 28
The paucity of research on the effects that media campaigns have on subjective states, along with the economy of such campaigns if shown to have some effects, argues for the need for extensive research on this form of mental health education.

Having reviewed the studies concerning attitudes and beliefs and those concerning subjective states, we close this chapter by noting the four studies in which the dependent variable is behavior or practices — what people do. Although few in number, they are consistent in that none shows positive results. The studies are the following.

Andrew *et al.* (1960), 1: Mothers who participated in a non-directive discussion group showed a non-significant trend toward more favorable ratings of their children's behavior problems.

Greenberg *et al.* (1962), 2: A large mailing of *Pierre the Pelican* pamphlets showed no effect on the child-handling practices of mothers.

Owings (1931), 3: A sex-education program showed changes in knowledge but no changes in practices.

Schaus (1932), 2: A parent-education course showed no significant effects on "home practices."

Because each of the four studies involves one particular kind of practice—child-rearing techniques—it is impossible to relegate the loss to the general inability of educational techniques to affect behavior. After all, people do learn to swim in physical education classes. Perhaps parental behavior is particularly resistant to change; perhaps change that involves a chain of behavior (that of the parent and the child) is harder to effect. In either case, we may be gratified that theoretical emphasis has shifted away from stress on child-rearing as a mental health problem, for the existing record is quite pessimistic.

CONCLUSION 29

Studies of attempts to modify the child-handling practices of mothers show generally negative results.

CONCLUSION

The results of this review of the literature are, in our judgment, disappointing. Although we found forty experiments, some successful and some unsuccessful, it proved almost impossible to tease out generalizations which held beyond a given study. Roughly speaking, the best that we can do in the way of generalizations are the following.

1. It appears that there is a continuum in degrees of change from beliefs to attitudes to subjective states to practices. At one extreme, almost all studies of change in information show positive results, while at the other, studies of change in practices show uniformly negative outcomes.
2. The most strategic target areas of mental health education, attitude and subjective-state changes, lie in the middle of this range, where both positive and negative effects are reported.

3. The diversity of studies and measures makes it almost impossible to speculate about the differences between successful and unsuccessful attempts.
4. A key assumption of existing mental health education programs — that mass exposure of books, pamphlets, movies, and so on, has a positive effect on subjective states — has not been, and should be, studied.

5

Conclusions
and
Recommendations

A mental health education program may be thought to consist of four major parts: (1) substantive content, (2) medium or vehicle, (3) audience, and (4) goal. A prototype is given in the tabulation below.

Our original assumption was that the major obstacles to success in conducting programs would turn up in the bottom three rows, specifically: (1) dependent variables would be difficult to measure; (2) audiences might be resistant to the information; (3) the delicacy of the content might require special techniques, such as discussions led by a psychiatrist. On the whole, this assumption was not borne out by our review of the literature. In fact, (1) omnibus inventories of mental health and ratings by experts appear to be no less efficient than other social-science measures; (2) audiences appear eager to receive mental health information because they have few firm existing ideas and a great interest in the area; and (3) simple mass-media techniques appear to be as efficient as more complicated and sophisticated vehicles for conveying information.

Rather, the major problem appears to be this: *mental health educators have little or nothing specific and practical to tell the public.* In stark generalizations:

1. The so-called principles of mental hygiene are vague slogans rather than strategies of behavior which can be put into practice.
2. The task of research findings is to challenge existing beliefs of

laymen ("big cities are bad for mental health") and professionals ("breast-feeding is good for mental health"), rather than to add positive generalizations.

3. Environmental and situational stresses play such an important part in determining generalized subjective distress that candid rules for mental health must include such advice as: "Do not be poor or ignorant, and stay out of armed combat."

4. There is no known method of preventing the major functional psychoses.

5. There are no known rules for influencing the emotional development of children.

6. Although basic research on these matters is increasing in quantity and quality, it is extremely unlikely that the situation will change much in the next decade, since progress will come from gradual accumulations of knowledge, not from a dramatic experimental breakthrough.

Shall we then abandon the task? Tempting as this alternative might be, we feel it is irresponsible. A human problem exists, and it is enormous. Getting even slight results is better than doing nothing. The research results do not tell us that subjective states are unmodifiable, they merely say that we cannot state principles for modifying them. The general population seeks information on adjustment and development, and the field should not be abandoned to quacks and popularizers. There has been no study of the effectiveness of mass campaigns aimed at the positive mental health of adults.

Furthermore, a somewhat more optimistic tone may be taken

Major Parts	Program A	Program B	Program C
Content	Principles of child development	Principles of child development	Principles of adjustment
Medium	Discussion groups	Movies	Pamphlets
Audience	Mothers	Mothers	Teen-agers
Goal	Improving mothers' techniques of child-rearing	Improving techniques of child-rearing	Improving personal adjustment

if we distinguish between "doing" and "understanding." We have assumed all along that principles of mental health are useful to the extent that they can be applied as a means to an end. Thus the principle that cigarette smoking causes cancer can be translated into a means-end rule: "If you want to avoid cancer, do not smoke cigarettes." However, the mental health principle that racial discrimination is associated with unhappiness cannot be translated into the means-end rule "If you want to be happy, do not be discriminated against." Nor can the mental health principle that there is no correlation between infant-care practices and children's personality be translated into the means-end rule "If you want your child to have a certain personality, either breast-feed him or do not."

However, we can make a case for the contention that information serves many functions other than that of a guide for doing. We note the following.

1. *Possessing information reassures people.* — Again, let us quote Nunnally (1961, p. 231).

People are evidently unsure of their information about mental health issues. Consequently, they will accept almost any seemingly authoritative and factual sounding information. The acceptance of new information, regardless of its validity, reduces the fear. . . .

2. *Information provides standards for evaluating one's self.* — A number of social psychological theories,[1] based on a wide variety of empirical findings, lead to the general conclusion that people tend to assess rewards and punishments not only in terms of their intrinsic hedonic value but also by comparison with standards based on the experience of others (reference groups and persons). The heart of this theory of "relative deprivation" can be conveyed by a classic example from the *American Soldier* studies. Although promotion rates for enlisted men were higher in the Air Force than in the Military Police, soldiers in the former tended to take a dimmer view of promotion

[1] See Merton and Kitt (1950), Festinger (1954), Davis (1959).

opportunities. Stouffer explains this by saying that, where promotion is common, the promoted soldier has not achieved so much relatively, and the non-promoted soldier has been relatively deprived. But where promotion rates are low, the promoted soldier sees himself as doing very well relatively, while the non-promoted soldier can console himself with the fact that many of his buddies are in the same boat.

What does this famous theory have to do with information? If it is true that people tend to evaluate their situations in terms relative to the situations of others, the conclusions they draw will be a function of the information available to them. *To the extent that people are misinformed about others, they will misjudge their own situations.*

Actually, we know very little about the accuracy with which we judge social facts, but what little evidence there is suggests that such judgments are far from accurate. The phenomenon in which "everyone" believes something, and is simultaneously convinced that he is alone in the belief, has been dubbed "pluralistic ignorance." The following are examples.

a) In a recent NORC survey of a national samples of college seniors, 67 per cent said they felt that the most important purpose of college was "a basic education and appreciation of ideas," but only 38 per cent said it was "most important to the typical student here."

b) Breed and Ktsanes (1961), in a study of a southern congregation, found that among those who perceived others' opinions, 43 per cent said they would quit or protest if the church were desegregated, while 70 per cent thought others would react this way.

c) Political polls, which treat an area where there is a tremendous flood of information, show the American public to be poorly informed. Thus the Gallup Poll in 1952 found that 31 per cent of a national sample did not know the name of the Vice-President of the United States (Alben Barkley). In 1952, 53 per cent could not give a correct answer to the question: "Will you tell me what the initials G.O.P. stand for? In 1961, 43 per cent did not know the answer to the question: "Would you tell me what is meant by the 'fall-out' of an H-bomb?"[2]

d) We remember from Chapter 3 that Fiedler found very low correlations between his subjective and objective measures of assumed similarity.

Taken together, the assumptions that self-judgments are heavily affected by perceived social norms, and that perceptions of social phenomena are only roughly accurate, lead to the hypothesis that the presentation of accurate information should have a definite effect on self-judgments.

3. *Information serves to inoculate against overreactions to stress.*—This proposition is the subject of a book-length discussion by Janis (1958) in his volume *Psychological Stress.* Attention is centered on emotional reactions to surgery, but Janis suggest that his argument is general. In paraphrase, his position is that if a group of people are going to be exposed to a stress situation, those who are uninformed before the stress, or those who pooh-pooh the forthcoming difficulties, will find the discrepancy between expectation and reality so great that they will become upset, while those who expected trouble all along will handle the situation more realistically. Thus, his thesis is "forewarned is forearmed."

Taken together, these three hypotheses suggest the following idea. Even though the causal dynamics are unknown and no rules for efficient action can be justified, merely exposing people to "Gesell norms" for strategic areas of their lives should have the following effects: (1) the feeling of possessing valid knowledge about the area should in itself be reassuring; (2) knowing how one realistically compares with others should lead to the elimination of unrealistic self-judgments based on inaccurate perceptions; and (3) knowledge of impending problems should serve to inoculate people against overreacting when the actual stress situation occurs.

At this point a major practical obstacle appears, for, with the exception of certain demographic variables reported in the United States Census, we do not have available the appro-

---

[2] A large number of such findings are reviewed by Erskine (1962).

priate normative data in the content areas relevant to mental health. For most of the important aspects of life, samples are grossly unrepresentative (e.g., Gesell's own norms), are limited to very small populations (Blood's [1960] data on Detroit or the Berkeley growth study [MacFarlane *et al.*, 1954]), or are not of sufficient size for reliable tabulations on small subgroups (*Americans View Their Mental Health*). Therefore, we suggest the following general strategy for a study of mental health education.

1. Survey some fairly large population, gathering data on specific problems, satisfactions, and environmental situations, as well as initial measures on the dependent variables.
2. Expose some, but not all, of the respondents to the results in the form of a popularly written description of the factual findings.
3. Resurvey, after a period of time, those subjects who received the informational feedback (experimentals) and those who did not (controls) to see whether there are any differences in terms of the dependent variables.

RECOMMENDATIONS FOR A MENTAL HEALTH EDUCATION RESEARCH STUDY: A FEEDBACK SURVEY

As set forth above, the feedback hypothesis is extremely general and could be applied to any population group. There is no reason in principle why such a study could not be carried out on a representative cross-section of the total American population.[3] However, the heterogeneity of the nation's population would require an enormous sample, diverse feedback programs for particular population groups, and high sampling and field costs. Thus, for technical as well as substantive reasons, we propose a study limited to grammar- and high-school children.

---

[3] A possible limit is that, according to the reference-group hypothesis, information on a given population should be effective only to the degree that the population is used as a reference group. The prediction is that an information campaign telling middle-aged Americans how they compare with Japanese teen-agers of the opposite sex would be less effective than a campaign telling them how they compare with people whom they routinely use for a reference group.

1. Technical considerations
   a) Because up to age fifteen some 90 per cent of the nation's children are in school, existing rosters of students provide a cheap sampling frame for a population that is quite representative.
   b) If school staffs are willing to cooperate (and because mental health is a topic of considerable concern to educators, we may assume almost unanimous cooperation) schedules may be administered efficiently and inexpensively through the school systems.
2. Substantive considerations
   a) Because young people's lives may be assumed to change more in a given period of time than do adults' lives, children can provide a test of the "inoculation" hypothesis more conveniently that adults (e.g., it might take ten years to test the effectiveness of information campaigns inoculating people against the stress of aging and retirement).
   b) We may assume that students use other students as their reference group, so the norms will probably be salient.
   c) If shown to be successful, such a program could be turned over to educators for practical application, remembering that schools reach more Americans for a longer period of time than any other formal institution in the society.
   d) Even if the action program proves to be a failure, the data generated can fill an important research gap, as we noted in Chapter 3.
   e) There is considerable literature indicating a complicated pattern of changes in worries and concerns by grade in school.[4]
   f) It may be assumed that gross environmental factors (health, unemployment, etc.) play a minor role in students' adjustment.

Let us now sketch the steps in such a research program in terms of sampling, initial measures, treatment, follow-ups, and analyses.

[4]See Pressey and Kuhlen (1957, pp. 338–53).

Sampling

In sketching the design we use the State of Pennsylvania as our universe. There would be no great obstacles and few differences in the design and cost if the study were to be carried out in another geographical area or throughout the total United States. The steps involved are the following:

1. Obtain a list of the schools in Pennsylvania and a reasonable estimate of the number of students enrolled in each grade from sixth to twelfth.

2. Stratify the schools in terms of size, size of city, and census measures of the SES of the community or neighborhood served by the school.

3. Set a total sample size. Assuming that the predicted effects are at best fairly slight, this sample size should be rather large, perhaps 30,000 cases.

4. Set a total for the number of schools to be included in the study. Because schools will be the treatment units, the number of schools should be rather large, perhaps one hundred per treatment.

We anticipate some difficulties at this point. Ideally, a "school" should consist of a single institution in which the same students progress from sixth grade through high-school graduation. The existence of junior high schools, schools whose students are not geographically recruited, etc., as well as multiple primary schools feeding a given secondary school, presents a number of conceptual problems which would have to be ironed out during the planning stage.

5. By the use of well-established multistage sampling procedures, sampling intervals can be established, giving a specified number of cases to be sampled in each school, the total cases in the study being representative of the students in the universe.

6. Within each sampled school, draw the "quota" of students by means of probability sampling from school records.

Initial Measures

7. Identical, brief schedules (except perhaps for different forms for boys and girls) are to be filled out by each student in the sample, except for a small fraction who will receive only a

"post-" measure. (This group enables one to determine whether the sheer filling-out of the original questionnaire contributed to any observed effects. This analysis is discussed in step 12 below.)

8. The content of the schedules should include the following. (*a*) A brief, omnibus (ten- to fifteen-item) mental health scale of the type discussed in Chapter 2. (*b*) A list of approximately thirty-five worries, concerns, and behaviors from existing scales, such as the Pressey Interest-Attitude test, or made up for this research. (1) An attempt should be made to cover each content area with two separate items, a "factual" and a "reaction" item, for example: "I go out on dates once a week or more" and "I worry about my popularity with the opposite sex"; "I usually miss two weeks or more during the school year because of illness" and "I am concerned about my health"; "I often worry whether my grades are good enough to get into college" and reported grade average. Each item is to be presented in three separate response frameworks: "true-false for me personally"; "your guess as to how *most* students you know will answer this" (T-F); and "how you guess you would answer this question one year from now" (T-F); and "how you guess you would answer this question one year from now" (T-F). These frameworks enable us to score students in terms of their subjective states, their perceived standing vis-à-vis their reference group, and their expectations regarding the future. (*c*) A brief set of background items: father's education, father's occupation, siblings, religion, length of time in this school, grade average or rank in class, race, school program, career plans. (*d*) A question asking whether student has taken a course in psychology, personal adjustment, mental hygiene, etc. This item can be used in two ways. First, in the final analysis, exposed students can be separated out to control for the influence of these courses. Second, some students may say "no" in the initial measure and "yes" on the follow-up, in which case their changes may be used to see the effects of such courses. (*e*) The students' home mailing addresses (for use in treatments). (*f*) A brief (possibly ten-item) true-and-false test concerning the content of the "advice" treatment described in step 10 below. The schedules should be completely precoded so that no coding or editing is necessary, and they may be key-punched immediately upon receipt.

Treatments

We propose two treatments, and two levels of each treatment, with schools randomly assigned to treatment groups.

9. *Treatment one (information).* — It is assumed that the pre-coded schedules can be keypunched, machine-edited, converted to computer tape, and key tables run on a high-speed computer within four months after the completion of the fieldwork. Basically the runs consist of tabulating the "me personally," "most students," and "year from now" responses for check-list items against grade in school, separately by sex, perhaps with controls for community type and/or father's education (SES).

The results should turn up finding on the order of the following: (*a*) major and minor concerns at particular grade levels; (*b*) patterns of increase and decrease over grades; (*c*) items characterized by "misperception" of reference groups (e.g., situations in which high percentages say they worry, and low percentages say "most students" worry; and (*d*) items characterized by "misperceptions" of future states (e.g., items showing discrepancies between "next year" for students in grade N and "me personally" in grade N + 1).

At this point, a professional writer and a commercial artist who have been hired on a consultant basis, working with the study director, prepare a series of perhaps half a dozen short, simply written, attractively illustrated pamphlets presenting the results to student readers (e.g., *What's in Store for You Next Year?* or *Teen-agers' Concerns* or *Are You Really Different?*). Although an attempt is made to "package" the results in a readable fashion and to suggest that they are "important," no specific advice or suggestions as to techniques for problem solution are to be presented. The pamphlets are mailed at a regular (weekly?) interval to the homes of students in the "information" treatment group, and the final mailing includes a return postal card with one or two questions on reactions, as a rough measure of penetration.

10. *Treatment two (advice).* — Students in the "advice" treatment group are to be mailed the same number of pamphlets at the same time but, instead of the information content described above, the pamphlets are selected from already existing pamphlets concerning students and student problems, of the sort already in plentiful supply from existing mental health education

programs. An attempt should be made to find a series appropriate to the grade levels involved, similar in attractiveness and format and giving heavy stress to classical mental health themes, rather than factual information.

11. *Treatment levels.* — In order to check for the differential effects of differences in "dosage," an attempt should be made to incorporate the two treatments into actual school programs at a small randomly selected fraction of the schools. The actual procedures will have to be carefully worked out (e.g., whether it is possible to incorporate the materials into regular courses in social studies or whether a special after-school class must be established) but the general aim is to have the students meet with a teacher for one period on each pamphlet, cover the materials in standard classroom fashion, and take a final examination. Actually, their "post-" measurement serves as a final examination for purposes of research, but a "real" examination would presumably have motivating properties. Assuming seven grade levels and five classes per grade level, thirty-five such intensive treatment groups are proposed for each treatment (information and advice), making a total of seventy.

The accompanying chart summarizes the design and indicates a tentative distribution of children and schools for each treatment. The size of the project appears tremendous, but it should be noted that NORC has successfully completed a panel study of

	Initial Questionnaire	
Treatment	Yes	No
None (controls)	10,000 students, 100 schools	1,000 students, 10 schools
Information — low intensity	10,000 students, 100 schools	500 students, 5 schools
Information — high intensity	1,050 students, 5 schools*	500 students, 5 schools
Advice — low intensity	10,000 students, 100 schools	500 students, 5 schools
Advice — high intensity	1,050 students, 5 schools*	500 students, 5 schools
Total	32,100 students, 310 schools	2,000 students, 20 schools
Grand total	34,100 students, 330 schools	

*Based on the following assumption: 30 students per class × 7 grade levels × 5 schools.

1961 college graduates with a sample of approximately 34,000 students from 135 colleges, without the advantage of classroom administration of the schedules.

Follow-up

12. One year after the initial measure, the same instrument should be administered to the total sample. The group that received no initial questionnaire fills out the schedule for the first time at this step and the remainder fill out their second. The operation appears to be straightforward, except for the problem of students in higher grades who leave school before graduation and for the fact that those in the twelfth grade at the first interview wave will have graduated. Two approaches can be taken to this problem. On the one hand, the existence of mailing addresses, and the high probability that the schools could help locate those whose mailing addresses are invalid, means that it may be possible to reach a very high proportion of these students by mail. On the other hand, there is justification for considering the dropouts "mortality," in the sense that the feedback information about eleventh graders given to tenth graders will be about eleventh graders who continued in school, not those who dropped out. This information is thus not entirely appropriate for the tenth grader who is going to leave school (whether he knows it or not), and his results are not entirely germane to the hypotheses being tested. Since, however, the characteristics and later adjustment of dropouts and graduates are of such high substantive interest, they undoubtedly should be followed. It should be noted, however, that even high loss rates do not vitiate the logic of the design.

Analyses

The data generated in the two waves should provide a rich store of information, even though the number of items in the schedule will be modest by the standards of contemporary survey research. At the worst, assuming that neither of the treatments has any effect on the group as a whole or on any significant subgroup, the data may then be treated as a simple representative sample of the universe and analyzed in terms of the following: (1) differentials in adjustment and subjective distress among adolescents and preadolescents by age and various subgroups; (2) stability and change in mental health states over a one-year period; (3) items predictive of leaving secondary school without graduating; (4) reference-group phenomena among adolescents; and (5) changes in plans for careers and advanced training, by grade in school and over a one-year time span, and by various background characteristics.

In terms of the analyses structured by the experimental design, the following questions may be answered.

1. Are there significant differences in the changes of the experimental groups in contrast with the control groups?

2. If yes: (*a*) Are there significant differences between the two treatment groups by specific items or by degree of change in a particular item? (*b*) Are there particular subgroups in the sample which show greater or smaller changes in various items or in amount of change? (*c*) Are there significant differences in the items changing, or is there frequency of change on a given item associated with levels of intensity for a given treatment? (*d*) If there are significant differences for treatment level, do the effects vary with students' characteristics?

3. Regarding the group which received no questionnaires in the initial wave, three comparisons are of particular interest: (*a*) a comparison between those of this group falling into "control" and the total sample in the first wave will give an estimate of cohort historical change — that is, the degree of difference between *n*th graders in subsequent years, regardless of the experiment; (*b*) a comparison between those of this group falling into "control" and the second wave results for controls measured twice will indicate the effect on the dependent variables of merely administering the questionnaire; (*c*) a comparison between this group and the appropriate treatment groups in the twice-measured will indicate the degree to which prior administration of the questionnaire enhances (perhaps sensitizes one to) or inhibits (perhaps creates resistance to) the effects; that is, whether prior questionnaire administration interacts with the treatment.

4. The inoculation hypothesis can be tested if chains of inference such as the following are supported empirically: (*a*) Let us assume that we find, as Pressey suggests, that worries about

examinations increase steadily from sixth grade to high-school graduation. (*b*) If, in the control group at the second wave, we found that students who expected exam pressures to decline (i.e., who checked "yes" for "me personally" and "no" for "next year" on a question about finding examinations hard) were more worried a year later than students who anticipated continued or increased pressures, Janis' general hypothesis would be confirmed — if it were also shown that exposure to the information treatments resulted in more realistic expectations, then (*c*) it would follow that the information treatment has an inoculating effect.

5. The reference-group hypothesis can be tested if chains of inference such as the following are supported empirically: (*a*) If students in the same objective circumstances (e.g., date irregularly) are more worried about their popularity when they believe that "most students" date more frequently, and if it turns out that dating by "others" is overestimated, and if exposure to the information treatment brings down the estimate for "most students," then (*b*) if would follow that the information treatment has the effect of reducing the negative effects of "pluralistic ignorance" on self-judgments.

6. The hypothesis of the "advice" treatment — that the acceptance of principles of mental hygiene is associated with im-

Phase	Required Time (Months)	Target Date, Assuming Project Begins January 1, 1965
1. Design, sampling, pretest of schedules, securing cooperation of sample schools	9	January–September, 1965
2. First field wave	1	October, 1964
3. Keypunching, tabulation, preparation of feedback materials	4	November, 1965 – February, 1966
4. Treatment mailing	1	March, 1966
5. Analysis of wave-1 data and preparation for second field wave	6	April–September, 1966
6. Second field wave	1	October, 1966
7. Keypunching, tabulations, analysis	14	November, 1966 – December, 1967
Total	36	

provement in adjustment — can be tested by determining whether improvement in scores on the ten-item test is associated with the "advice" treatment and with improvements in adjustment, and, if so, whether there is any significant advantage for the "advice" group when their second-wave information scores are held constant.

Timing and Budget

We anticipate that such a study could be conducted with the time schedule given in the accompanying tabulation. We have not prepared detailed budget estimates on this preliminary design. But it is our impression, from experience with similar projects, that total costs would be on the order of $175,000. The heaviest expeditures would occur during the first (sampling and first field wave) and second (treatment and second field wave) years, with a considerable drop in costs during the final year of analysis and writeup.

Annotated
Bibliography

The following is a systematic commentary on the experimental studies considered in Chapter 4. (For explanation of annotation procedures, see pp. 124–26). For convenience, all entries are also given in the References.

ANDREW, G. A study of the effectiveness of a workship method for mental health education. *Ment. Hygiene*, 1954, **38**, 627–33.

Population: Parents, teachers, public health nurses, and college students in the upper peninsula of Michigan.
Treatment: Two-day workshop using phonograph records, lectures, films, discussions on mental health topics.
Dependent variables: Thirty-item test of information and items measuring reactions to hypothetical situations; Hovland Effectiveness Index used to assess change.
Treatment groups: E: Before-and-after measures on workshop participants. C: Two measures on "people of different backgrounds who were in college."
Results: Improvement in experimentals significantly greater than that in controls, and experimentals improved on twenty-one out of thirty items.
Deficiencies: No evidence that experimentals and controls were similar to begin with; impossible to determine from the report which, if any, differences were associated with particular media (discussions, lectures, etc.).
Over all: Course × attitudes and beliefs: +.

ANDREW, G., SIBILIO, J. P., and STEHMAN, V. Utility of the small group discussion method as practiced in certain applied settings. 1. Instrumental goal achievement of a mental health group. *Amer. J. publ. Hlth,* 1960, **50**, 785–90.

Population: Mothers of preschool children who volunteered for project.
Treatment: Non-directive group discussion.
Dependent variables: (1) Mothers' ratings of children's behavior

(temper, care of property, capacity to occupy self, cooperation in routines, etc.) as observed, preferred by mother, and as mothers perceive experts' evaluations. (2) Check-list of alternative reactions to sixteen common problems of child-rearing.

Treatment groups: E: Three groups of eight mothers, meeting once a week for ten weeks (final N = 14), measured before and after. C: Thirteen participants in an undescribed "YWCA program" measured at one and ten weeks.

Results: No significant differences, although direction of differences in problem check-list favored experimentals.

Deficiencies: No evidence on comparability of experimentals and controls; very small numbers of cases mean that only very strong effects could be statistically significant.

Over all: (1) Interaction × beliefs and attitudes: *?* (2) Interaction × practices: *?*

ASCH, M. J. Non-directive teaching in psychology: An experimental study. *Psychol. Monogr.*, 1951, **65** (No. 4).

Population: Male second-semester general psychology students at Mohawk College (upstate New York), in spring semester, 1948. All were World War II veterans.

Treatment: Non-directive ("student-centered") college course in psychology.

Dependent variables: (1) Knowledge—final exam scores in the course, (2) Bogardus Social Distance scale for various nationality and social groupings, (3) MMPI—blind ratings of "adjustment" of profile results, (4) Ratings of reactions to course.

Treatment groups: E: Twenty-three cases selected at registration (not clear whether selected at random) chosen to exclude anyone with previous experience in such a course and to have equal numbers from first-semester sections of various psychology instructors. C: 101 students enrolled in other conventionally taught sections of the same course. Various cases used in various analyses, depending on variables chosen for equating experimentals and controls. Note: both groups were assigned the same conventional textbook.

Results: (1) Knowledge—experimentals did significantly worse. (It should be noted that experimentals knew their examination had no effect on their final grades.) (2) Social distance—both groups showed lessened social distance, but experimentals no more than controls. (3) MMPI—73 per cent of experimentals rated as "better adjusted" in posttest in comparison with 23 per cent of twenty-two controls; difference highly significant. (4) Reactions to course—experimentals liked the course better but no difference in "helping to know myself better."

Deficiencies: No very important deficiencies, except that it is unclear in the nature of the design which aspect of the experimental treatment produced the results—the leader, the other students, the fact that the experimentals were told that their section was an innovation, the fact that students assigned their own final grades.

Over all: (1) Interaction × attitudes and beliefs: ? (vis-à-vis conventional teaching, although there was undoubtedly some increase in experimentals' knowledge of psychology). (2) Interaction × subjective states: +.

BALSER, B. H., BROWN, F., BROWN, M. L., JOSEPH, E. D., and PHILLIPS, D. K. Preliminary report on a controlled mental health workshop in a public school system. *Amer. J. Psychiat.*, 1955, **112,** 199–205.

Population: Teachers and school administrators in New Rochelle, New York, and an unnamed control school system.

Treatment: Fifteen lectures of half-hour duration by a psychiatrist on "normal personality development, mechanisms of defense," etc., followed by one-hour discussions.

Dependent variables: Measures of knowledge, pencil-and-paper measures of personal adjustment.

Treatment groups: E: (1) Thirty-eight volunteer teachers, (2) nineteen volunteer administrators. C: Two similar groups, matched in age, sex, grade taught, etc., in a different school system. Controls were informed that they were serving as controls.

Results: (*a*) Neither experimentals nor controls showed a significant increase in knowledge. (*b*) *Both* experimentals and controls showed significant increases on about half the adjustment measures. The authors interpret this as a "Hawthorne effect."

Deficiencies: As noted by the authors, the fact that both experimentals and controls showed increases in adjustment measures, along with the fact that controls were informed of the purpose of the study, suggests that the changes were not due to the course but to the subjects' reactions to participation in the study.

Over all: (1) Course × attitudes and beliefs: −. (2) Course × subjective states: −.

BALSER, B. H., BROWN, F., BROWN, M. L., and LASKI, L. Further report on experimental evaluation of mental hygiene techniques in school and community. *Amer. J. Psychiat.*, 1957, **113**, 733 – 39.

Population: Groups of parents, groups of teachers, and parent-teacher groups in four New York metropolitan area communities.
Treatment: Lecture-discussion courses.
Dependent variables: Minnesota Personality Scales ("Morale," "Social Adjustment," "Family Relations," "Emotional Stability"); sentence completion measure of tension and adjustment; scale measuring "liberalism" in parent-child relations.
Treatment groups: Seven lecture-discussion groups formed according to the following design.

Population	Treatment	Leader	N
Experimentals:			
Teachers	Leader-centered discussion	Psychiatrist	20
Teachers	Leader-centered discussion	Psychologist	11
Parents	Group-centered discussion	Psychiatrist	11
Controls:			
Parents	Informed of nature of study		25
Teachers	Not informed of nature of study ("blind")		50
Parents	Not informed of nature of study ("blind")		20
Teachers	Not informed of nature of study ("blind")		8

Results: As shown in the following tabulation.

	Five Measures of Adjustment			
	Zero or Unfavorable Change	Positive Change Not Significant	Positive Change Significant at .05 Level	Total Tests
Three experimental groups	3	10	2	15
Informed controls	3 } 11	2 } 8	0 } 1	5
Blind controls	8	6	1	15
	Liberalism in Parent-Child Relations			
Three experimental groups	0	1	2	3
Informed controls	1 } 2	0 } 2	0	1
Blind controls	1	2	0	3

Deficiencies: Small sizes of groups mean that only the strongest possible changes could be statistically significant.

Over all: Although only four out of a possible fifteen tests on changes in adjustment showed a significant increase for the experimentals, when all the tests and groups are pooled we get the following, ignoring levels of significance.

Changes in Adjustment		
	Zero or Negative	Positive
Experimentals	3	12
Controls	11	9

By Fisher's exact test, this table is significant at the .05 level. Hence, the experimentals tended to show more improvement. (1) Course × attitudes and beliefs: +. (2) Course × subjective states: +.

BERKOWITZ, L. *Aggression: A social psychological analysis.* New York: McGraw-Hill Book Co., 1962.

Chapter 8, "Catharsis" (pp. 196–228) is an extensive review of a considerable number of complex experimental studies and thus cannot be cited in the outline form applicable to the other references in this section. On the basis of his own and other experiments, however, Berkowitz is led to question strongly the assumption of some mental health educators that the expression of aggression (as opposed to "bottling it up") has positive results. The following quotations provide examples. "There is no conclusive evidence one way or another as to the consequences of aggressive contests. Nevertheless, such findings as are available seem to point to an aggression-anxiety (and/or guilt) reaction to these games rather than pleasant feelings following the discharge of hostile impulses" (p. 204). "Expressing aggression does not in itself lessen the probability of further aggressive acts. Aggressive habits may even be reinforced" (p. 207). "Overt hostility is relatively unlikely to weaken to any great extent if an obstacle to need satisfaction continues to elicit anger" (p. 211). "Some people advocate the free expression of feelings when barely submerged resentment impedes harmonious relationships. . . . Unfortunately, however, such a philosophy sometimes leads to enhanced anger. Mutual recriminations may develop. . . . But more than this, when a person vents his feelings he may also excite himself even more" (p. 213). "In general there is no unequivocal evidence of a cathartic lessening in the strength of aggressive tendencies following the performance of hostile acts. Such a phenomenon may well exist, but the studies that have been conducted to date have not been altogether convincing" (p. 219). *Over all:* Miscellaneous × subjective states: −.

BRUCE, P. Relationship of self-acceptance to other variables with sixth grade children oriented in self-understanding. *J. educ. Psychol.*, 1958, **49**, 229 – 38.

A further report from this study, giving essentially similar results for a smaller sample, appears in R. E. MUSS. The effects of a one and two-year causal learning program. *J. Pers.*, 1960, pp. 479 – 91.

Population: Sixth-grade students in different elementary schools in a Midwestern community of 80,000.
Treatment: "Causally oriented" teaching program.
Dependent variables: Discrepancy in rating of self and ideal self; children's manifest anxiety scale; Kooker Security-Insecurity Rating Scale.
Treatment groups: (a) Experimental classes exposed to weekly program oriented toward "causal" approach to human problems with specially trained teachers: two classes exposed two years; two classes exposed one year. (b) Control classes matched on sex, IQ, teacher type, etc., and given no special program.
Results: At testing, experimental showed significant advantage ($p < .05$) on manifest anxiety and Kooker scales but not on discrepancy rating.
Deficiencies: No obvious ones, although data are all "after" rather than "before-after."
Over all: Course × subjective states: +.

CUMMING, E., and CUMMING, J. *Closed ranks: An experiment in mental health education.* Cambridge, Mass.: Harvard University Press, 1957.

Population: Two communities (populations 1,500 and 1,100) in central Canada.

Treatment: Six-month intensive campaign. Front-page stories in local newspaper, series of PTA programs, weekly radio program, three-day mental health film festival, speeches to local conventions, five meetings with older high-school students, pamphlets put on display in public buildings, books given to public library, study group established, etc.

Dependent variables: Guttman scales measuring (*a*) "Social distance" — how close a relationship the respondent is prepared to tolerate with someone who has been mentally ill. (*b*) "Social responsibility" — covers two possible ideas, responsibility for causing mental illness as well as responsibility for assuming the social burden which the mentally ill person places on society (cf. p. 54).

Treatment groups: Campaign conducted in one community, both communities surveyed before and after. Total adult population in experimental community, 107 randomly selected adults in control city.

Results: (*a*) "Fifty-six per cent of those interviewed in experimental community had had some contact with the program and were aware of its content, but these people were concentrated in the upper and medium rental areas" (p. 32). (*b*) "The average scores on our two Guttman scales had not changed. . . . The experimental community did not show any move in score which distinguished it from the control community, although one section of the population — the most highly educated — did, after the project, have a more polarized opinion regarding responsibility for mental illness . . . the occurrence of more high and low scores with an unchanged average" (p. 87).

Deficiencies: Many possible dependent variables were not explored; in particular, none of the standard measures of adjustment.

Over all: Media × attitudes and beliefs: −.

FIEDLER, F. E. An experimental approach to preventive psychotherapy. *J. abnorm. and soc. Psychol.*, 1949, **44,** 386–93.

Population: University of Chicago undergraduates.

Treatment: Non-directive group therapy to reduce anxiety about examinations.

Dependent variables: Ten-item graphic self-rating scale. Sample items: "more, less, or about as nervous, jittery, restless"; "Many students sleep poorly and toss and turn the nights immediately preceding an exam. How did you fare?"

Treatment groups: (*a*) Requested volunteers for a study on "whether nervousness, anxiety, etc. before an examination can be effectively reduced by organized group discussions." (*b*) Volunteers randomized as follows: E: Twenty-five cases randomly assigned to five groups with four different leaders, met fifty minutes per week for six weeks. C: Nineteen cases.

Results: "No significant differences were obtained when all experimental subjects were compared with all control subjects on any item or on the total scale."

Deficiencies: (*a*) Small sample size makes it difficult to get statistically significant results except for very strong effects. (*b*) Data presented in article show that scores on adjustment index increase with grades, and while grades were not associated with return of second-time schedules among experimentals, there was a sharp loss of control cases with low grades. The net result is that control cases have higher grades than experimentals. When experimentals are compared with controls with similar grades, experimentals have more favorable scores, but case bases are very small.

Over all: Interaction × subjective states: ?.

FORD, M., and HARTMAN, E. E. Measuring reader comprehension of a preschool pamphlet. *Publ. hlth Reps.*, 1954, **69**, 498 – 502.

Population: Working mothers (aged twenty to twenty-nine) of small children in Minneapolis, Minnesota, whose children were in four day-care centers in low-income neighborhoods.

Treatment: Preliminary version of a pamphlet regarding "contributions of parents and others in the emotional growth and development of the child," reasons for preschool physical and dental examinations, immunization, "sound health practices and habits," training for safety.

Dependent variables: Scores on ten-item multiple-choice examination on content of pamphlet.

Treatment groups: On a given Friday, every other mother was given pamphlet and asked to take it home and read it. Both experimentals and controls retested on following Monday. For experimentals, N = 21; for controls, N = 14.

Results: Significant difference ($p < .001$); experimental mean = 6.4, control = 3.7.

Deficiencies: None of practical importance. Authors do not report results for separate items, hence, one cannot tell results for specific mental health questions. Implication from the text, however, is that all ten items were in same favorable direction.

Over all: Media × attitudes and beliefs: +.

GREENBERG, B. G., HARRIS, M. E., MACKINNON, C. F., and CHIPMAN, S. S. A method for evaluating the effectiveness of health education literature. *Amer. J. publ. Hlth*, 1953, **43,** 1147 – 55.

Population: Mothers of first-born children in North Carolina.

Treatment: Pierre the Pelican pamphlets on child-rearing techniques.

Dependent variables: Personal-interview data on mothers' beliefs and practices regarding reactions to refusing food, demand-feeding, appropriate age for drinking from a glass, use of a bottle propped on a pillow, self-feeding.

Treatment groups: Experimentals and controls chosen randomly from registration records of first births in randomly selected counties. Experimentals (N = 1,156) received complete set of pamphlets through mail. Controls (N = 1,043) received nothing.

Results: (*a*) Experimentals tended to like the pamphlets – 100 per cent of 51 per cent return on postcard query was favorable. (*b*) No significant differences in the five attitude-practice areas.

Deficiencies: None; a technically excellent study.

Over all: (1) Media × attitudes and beliefs: –. (2) Media × practices: –.

LETON, D. A. An evaluation of group methods in mental hygiene. *Ment. Hygiene*, 1957, **41,** 525 – 33.

Population: Ninth-graders in four high schools in St. Paul, Minnesota; students with initially very low scores on Bell Adjustment Inventory excluded.

Treatments: (1) Bullis Human Relations Classes (a didactic mental health program for school children, described by Kotinsky and Witmer [1955]). (2) Mental hygiene movies. (3) Sociodrama and role-playing. (4) Hobby and crafts activities.

Dependent variables: Bell Adjustment Inventory, Bell School Inventory, Rogers Test of Personality Adjustment, grades and attendance records.

Treatment groups: (*a*) Over two years, six classes (thirteen students each) were assigned to Bullis Classes, six to movies, four to sociodrama, four to hobby and crafts. (*b*) Each experimental group met weekly for one semester with leaders chosen for good relationships with students and experience with the treatments. (*c*) Each experimental group was assigned a comparison control class of thirteen students.

Results: No consistent significant differences between changes of experimentals and controls for any of the four treatments.

Deficiencies: None of any importance; a very well-conducted study.

Over all: (1) Course × subjective states: −. (2) Media × subjective states: −. (3) Interaction × subjective states: −. (4) Miscellaneous subjective states: −. It is possible, however, that the exclusion of children originally very low in adjustment removed the group most likely to benefit from the programs.

McGINNIES, E., LANA, R., and SMITH, C. The effects of sound films on opinions about mental illness in community discussion groups. *J. appl. Psychol.*, 1958, **42,** 40–46.

Population: Members of PTA and child study groups in Prince Georges County, Maryland; two-thirds of housewives had average education of two to three years' college; average age, thirty-eight to thirty-nine.

Treatments: (1) Series of mental health films. (2) Half-hour discussion led by a trained psychologist following the films.

Dependent variables: Mental Health Opinion Inventory of forty-seven items (e.g., "It is better not to discuss a mental illness as I would a physical illness"; "Few of the people who seek psychiatric help need the treatment").

Treatment groups: Groups assigned as follows (N's indicated in cells).

Measured Before and After		
Films	Discussion	
	No	Yes
All 3 at bi-weekly intervals	16,18	13,11
C only	11	11
B only	13	8
A only	13	8
None	9,9	

For example, two groups, consisting of sixteen and eighteen members each, saw all three movies but had no discussion; two groups of nine members each served as controls, etc.

Results:

Mean Change Before and After		
Films	Discussion	
	No	Yes
All 3 at bi-weekly intervals	+15.4*	+16.4*
C	+ 4.6	− 1.2
B	+14.5	+ 1.9
A	+ 0.4	+ 6.1
None	+ 0.5	

*Significant increase between "before" and "after" and significantly higher than controls. All other cells not significant.

Conclusions: (*a*) While seeing one movie makes little difference, a series of three results in improved scores. (*b*) Discussions neither add to nor detract from the other effects.

Deficiencies: None; a well-designed, well-executed study.

Over all: (1) Media × attitudes and beliefs: +. (2) Interaction × attitudes and beliefs: − (since there was no group having a discussion and no movie, we can only interpret the effect of discussion as a supplement to movies).

MICHIGAN STATE DEPARTMENT OF HEALTH. *A report of some aspects of the effectiveness of the Pierre the Pelican mental health pamphlets.* Lansing: Michigan State Dept. of Health, 1952. (Mimeographed.)

Not found. Abstract is taken from Orville Brim's *Education for Child Rearing* (New York: Russell Sage Foundation, 1959, p. 298).

Population: Mothers of newly registered first births in certain Michigan counties.

Treatment: Pierre the Pelican pamphlets mailed to mothers.

Dependent variable: "43-item questionnaire based on the pamphlet materials."

Treatment groups: E: 477 returns from 1,000 cases. C: 537 returns from 1,000 cases. Difference: not clear from Brim; apparently counties were allocated to treatments—randomly, it is hoped—and all subjects in a given county fell into the treatment group.

Results: (a) At .05 level: eight favored experimentals, thirty-three "no difference," two favored controls (total of forty-three items). (b) Total number "correct" out of forty-three, $.10 > p > .05$. (c) Twenty-three items "involving some understanding beyond simple factual information," $p < .03$.

Deficiencies: Low return rate of questionnaires means that effects on non-respondents could alter the outcome considerably. Content of questionnaire unclear in Brim's abstract.

Over all: Media × attitudes and beliefs: ?.

NUNNALLY, J. C., JR. *Popular conceptions of mental health: Their development and change.* New York: Holt, Rinehart, and Winston, 1961.

A number of different experiments are reported in this book, as follows.

(1) Pages 150–58 (study designed and conducted by T. R. HUSEK):

Population: Five classes of high-school juniors and seniors, none of whom were taking courses in psychology or mental hygiene.

Treatments: (a) Certainty versus tentativeness in mental health information on cures for mental illness. (b) Messages "destructive" of beliefs regarding efficacy of cures for mental illness.

Dependent variables: Semantic differential measures of (a) understandability; (b) evaluation; (c) potency of (1) psychiatrist, (2) mental patient, (3) tranquilizing drugs, (4) mental illness, (5) ways of treating mental patients, (6) "me," (7) a person who has schizophrenia.

Treatment groups: (*a*) Subjects were randomly exposed to various one-page messages about mental illness therapy varying in certainty (e.g., "Years of research are beginning to pay off in valid conclusions" versus "Years of research are beginning to pay off but only in tentative conclusions") and control messages about non-mental-health topics. Semantic differential completed immediately after reading. (*b*) Two weeks later, same subjects received messages contradicting previous message, and then repeated semantic differential measures.

Results: (*a*) High-certainty treatment associated with more favorable ratings of mental health concepts. (*b*) In control groups which had not received original message, negation messages had the effect of making attitudes less favorable. (*c*) Negation effects were no "worse" in experimental groups which had received previous "positive" information.

Deficiencies: None

Over all: Media × attitudes and beliefs: +.

(2) Pages 158–61, 201–7 (study designed and conducted by T. R. HUSEK):

Population: 135 high-school juniors and seniors attending a particular school different from the school in (1)

Treatment: Same high- and low-certainty messages as in (1).

Dependent variable: Mean evaluation score on semantic differential ratings of mental health concepts, as in (1).

Treatment groups: Treatments randomized as in (1) and semantic differential administered (*a*) immediately after, (*b*) two weeks later, and (*c*) ten weeks after original measurement.

Results: (*a*) High-certainty messages more effective in creating positive attitudes than low certainty. (*b*) Low certainty more effective than control message. (*c*) Differences still significant at end of ten-week interval. (*d*) Controls increased in evaluation on third administration (possibly due to effect of semantic differential itself).

Deficiencies: None.

Over all: Media × attitudes and beliefs: +.

(3) Pages 161–64:

Population: Undergraduates at University of Illinois.

Treatment: Negation (contradiction) of messages regarding mental illness.

Dependent variables: Mean evaluation on semantic differential ratings of mental health concepts as in (1).

Treatment groups: E1 (N =30) read a one-page psychogenic explanation of catatonic schizophrenia, last paragraph of which denied validity of the explanation. E2 (N = 30): same as E1 but for physiogenic explanation. Two control groups of thirty persons read messages on Great Barrier Reef and use of typewriter. All four groups were administered semantic differential immediately after reading.

Results: Experimental groups less favorable to mental health concepts: "If you tell an individual that information about mental illness is incorrect and do not tell him what is correct, you will promote negative attitudes toward concepts like mental patient, psychiatrist, and methods of treating mental patients."

Deficiencies: None.

Over all: Media × attitudes and beliefs: +.

(4, 5) Pages 176–81 (study designed and conducted by E. E. WARE):

Population: High-school students (no other information given).

Treatment: Information regarding mental illness and prevention.

Dependent variables: (a) Information regarding topics covered.
(b) Attitudes toward psychiatrist, mental patient, mental hospital, etc., measured by semantic differential.

Treatment groups: 330 students randomly assigned to the following treatments. (a) Message claiming mental illness can be treated successfully. (b) Message claiming avoidance of morbid thoughts does not prevent mental illness. (c) Message claiming mental illness is not due to loss of will power. (d) Message denying that mental patients "look and act different." (e) Controls: No message. Dependent variables measured immediately after reading.

Results: (a) Information increased as predicted, changes being specific to the topic in the message. (b) Attitude changes were mixed favorable and unfavorable.

Deficiencies: None.

Over all: (a) Media × attitudes and beliefs: +. (b) Media × attitudes and beliefs: −.

(6) Pages 197–201, 222:

Population: Students in two high schools.

Treatment: Mental hygiene and psychology courses.
Dependent variables: (*a*) Information regarding mental health and illness. (*b*) Attitudes toward psychiatrist, mental patient, mental hospital, etc., as measured by semantic differential.
Treatment groups: School A: Thirty-six students from three sections of psychology course measured at beginning and end of semester and one year after completion of course. School B: Sixty-seven students from four sections of psychology course measured at beginning and end of semester and six months after end of semester. School A: Fifty-eight students in art course measured at beginning and end of semester (controls).
Results: Information—both experimentals and controls improved during the semester, but different items changed in different schools. Attitudes—both experimentals and controls developed more favorable attitudes toward mental health concepts during semester.
Deficiencies: As both experimentals and controls received same measurements, it is impossible to tell whether increases came from the questionnaire or from outside influences to which both were exposed or from spread of information from experimentals to controls.
Over all: Media × attitudes and beliefs: ?.

(7) Pages 225–30:

Population: University of Illinois students.
Treatment: False information about causes of catatonic schizophrenia.
Dependent variable: Attitudes toward catatonic schizophrenia, as measured by semantic differential.
Treatment groups: Six written messages randomly assigned to 192 students, as follows: Explanation of catatonic schizophrenia: (*a*) Psychogenic—plausible (parental rejection). (*b*) Psychogenic—implausible ("persona phobia"). (*c*) Physical—plausible ("substance in the blood"). (*d*) Physical—implausible (blocking of brain artery). (*e*) Control message (Great Barrier Reef). (*f*) Control message (typewriting).
Results: (*a*) All four treatments associated with more favorable attitudes toward catatonic schizophrenia than control messages. (*b*) No differences among the four treatments.
Deficiencies: None.
Over all: Media × attitudes and beliefs: +.

OJEMANN, R. H. Sources of infection revealed in preventive psychiatry research. *Amer. J. publ. Hlth*, 1960, **50**, 329 – 35.

Population: Fourth, fifth, and sixth graders in a midwestern city of 80,000.

Treatment: Experimental classroom teaching program.

Dependent variable: Test consisting of twenty-two human-relations problem situations, scored (negatively) in terms of the number of situations which the child would approach in "an arbitrary, punitive way."

Treatment groups: (*a*) Fourth-, fifth-, and sixth-grade classes exposed to weekly "causally oriented teaching content" and teachers given four-week summer training session; measured at beginning and end of year. (*b*) Control classes matched on IQ, age, sex, and experience and education of teachers; measured in fall and spring.

Results: Significant (*p* < .01) advantage in improvement for experimentals.

Deficiencies: None of any importance. Author notes that control teachers got more improvement when in the following year they served as experimentals, a finding which argues against teacher selection as a biasing factor.

Overall: Course × attitudes and beliefs: +.

OWINGS, C. *Studies in parental sex education.* Minneapolis, Minn.: University of Minneapolis Press, 1931.

Population: Mothers of children fourteen or younger in Minneapolis and St. Paul, Minnesota, during the late 1920's.

Treatment: Sex-education program involving a personal interview (by women volunteers not necessarily trained in mental hygiene) with each mother, during which volunteer gave "upon request" specific sex-education information, left pamphlets, and attempted to interest mother in local neighborhood discussion groups on sex education

Dependent variables: Several reported, but in essence the data reflect measures involving eighteen "scientific terms" (breast, nipples, navel, buttocks, rectum, uterus, penis, etc.). (1) Knowledge – mother's statement that she understands the term. (2) Attitudes — mother's rating of "desirability" and "objectionability" of use of the terms. (3) Practice — mother's report of the use of the terms by her children and between children and parents. Some data gathered from children themselves, but reporting is unclear.

Treatment groups: Experimentals: Every home in "a district selected for it economic stability and the educational advantages of the group living in it. . . . The 494 blocks included in the area selected was a fair cross-section of the city . . . mothers asked to fill out schedules after exposure to program. . . ." Controls: Neighborhood in St. Paul similar in socio-economic composition but not involved in program. Control families matched by pairing with experimentals *re* number, age, and sex of children, religion, father's occupation, mother's education, mother's age, type of home and neighborhood, parents' birthplace. After matching and exclusion of cases with missing data, analysis N's were 235 in each group.

Results: Although the research was apparently conducted with great care and a high level of technical skill, the report of the research is hopelessly disorganized and jumbled, and it is almost literally impossible to run down a number of details. It is our impression, however, that the data support the author's conclusions that "On six different items in knowledge content there are significant differences . . . favorable to Group B [experimentals]. There are no significant differences in any of the items pertaining to attitude. There are slight differences in three of the six items pertaining to practice, and in one a significant difference favorable to Group B."

Over all: (1) Miscellaneous × attitudes and beliefs: +. Information: ?. (2) Miscellaneous × attitudes and beliefs: −. Practices: ?. (3) Miscellaneous practices: −. Attitudes: −.

PRUGH, D. G., STAMB, E. M., SANDS, H. M., KIRSCHBAUM, R. M., and LENIHAN, E. A. A study of the emotional reactions of children and families to hospitalization and illness. *Amer. J. Orthopsychiat.*, 1953, **22,** 70 – 106.

Population: Children two to twelve years old hospitalized at Children's Medical Center, Boston.
Treatment: "Included daily visiting periods for parents, early am-

bulation of patients where medically feasible, a special play program employing a nursery-school teacher, psychological preparation for and support during potentially traumatic diagnostic or
therapeutic procedures, an attempt at clearer definition and in-
tegration of the parent's role in the care of the child, and other
[*sic*] techniques."

Dependent variables: Rating of child's adjustment during and
after hospitalization.

Treatment groups: Fifty experimental cases and fifty controls
matched to experimentals on age, sex, diagnosis and "other
factors," controls being treated in then existing routine of the
hospital.

Results: Experimentals showed considerably less severe reactions,
as follows:

Reaction	Control (Per Cent)	Experimental (Per Cent)
Severe	36	14
Moderate	56	54
Minimal	8	32
Total	100	100
N	50	50

Deficiencies: Treatment is so complex that it is impossible to determine whether any particular aspect of it had a positive effect.
Raters obviously knew which subjects were experimentals and
which were controls. Ward staff was undoubtedly aware of study
and motivated to help it succeed.

Over all: Miscellaneous × subjective states: +.

ROGERS, J. Operant conditioning in a quasi-therapy setting. *J. abnorm.
and soc. Psychol.*, 1960, **60**, 247–52.

Population: Male undergraduates in psychology course at Stanford University.

Treatment: Operant conditioning ("uh huh" and nodding).

Dependent variables: Taylor Manifest Anxiety Scale, adjective
self-description, sentence completion, Rogers and Diamond
Q-Sort Emotional Adjustment Test.

Treatment groups: Each subject received six ten-minute interviews with experimenter and was asked to describe spontaneously his personality characteristics and traits. In initial interview experimenter showed no reaction; in interviews two through six following reinforcement (simultaneous nodding and saying "uh huh"), groups were established as follows: (*a*) positive self-references reinforced, (*b*) negative self-references reinforced, and (*c*) no reinforcement.

Results: Significant changes vis-à-vis first interview. Group *a:* no significant change in content; group *b:* positive references declined, negative increased; group *c:* positive references declined. No change in dependent-variable measures.

Deficiencies: None, except that unrepresentative nature of the sample limits capacity to generalize; twenty-two of twenty-four cases reported they were unaware of conditioning.

Over all: Behavior (mentioning various types of content) by and large significantly affected in predicted directions; no change in subjective states. Therefore, miscellaneous × subjective states: −.

ROSE, A. M. Mental health attitudes of youth as influenced by a comic strip. *Journalism Quart.*, 1958, **35,** 333–42.

Population: Entire sophomore class in three Minneapolis, Minnesota, high schools.

Treatment: Reading episodes concerning onset and cure of a mild case of paranoia in comic strip "Rex Morgan, M.D." in *Minneapolis Tribune.* (The comic strip is written by a psychiatrist.)

Dependent variables: Information and attitude items regarding mental illness and mental patients (e.g., "The mentally ill are dangerous"; "Mentally ill can become completely well"; "Mental patients can become completely well").

Treatment groups: All cases measured a week or so after beginning of the episode (but before theme would become apparent to a layman) and several months later, after its end. Experimentals are self-designated readers of the strip; controls are self-designated non-readers. Analysis based on random subsample of 300 experimentals and 300 controls out of 1,190 cases.

Results: Both groups tended to shift in favorable direction on items directly covered in the strip. Experimental shifts were stronger and more often significant.

Deficiencies: Non-readers of the strip may be systematically different in many ways—less intelligent, less interested in medical and interpersonal content, etc. On the other hand, true differences may be obscured by word-of-mouth communication from readers to non-readers. Since, however, results are consistent with Nunnally's more carefully controlled experiments, findings are accepted. Design does not control for effects of measurement instrument, which may interact with strip (i.e., strip might not have influenced experimentals if their interest had not been raised by first measurement).

Over all: Media × attitudes, beliefs: +.

SCHAUS, H. S. An experimental investigation of methods in parent education. In K. W. HATTENDORF *et al.* (Eds.) *Researches in parent education. I.* ("University of Iowa Studies in Child Welfare," Vol. 6.) Iowa City, Iowa: University of Iowa, 1932, pp. 117–34.

Population: Mothers in existing child-study groups in Davenport, Iowa.

Treatments: Courses (lecture or study-discussion) meeting every other week for ten sessions, two devoted to before-and-after measures, eight devoted to topics such as the optimum child, aspects of discipline, food adjustment, play, books and reading, habit formation, fear, sex, education.

Dependent variables: (*a*) "Home practices in parent behavior," based on mother's questionnaires. (*b*) Information tests on content of course.

Treatment groups: (*a*) Six groups recruited from members of nine extant study groups (N's from 8 to 19). (*b*) Three assigned to lecture only, three assigned to discussions led by teacher; assignment "arbitrary." (*c*) At end, analysis groups selected from those who attended three or more times and for whom there were complete data; group matched on education, first scores, and age of children. N's not given, but apparently: *b*—Lecture (N = 28); *c*—Discussion (N = 27).

Results: (*a*) Home practices "only slightly higher." (*b*) Information: apparently both increased considerably, and at second measurement, discussion group was slightly higher, apparently significant at the .04 level.

Deficiencies: Reporting is rather unclear (remembering, of course, that the study was done thirty years ago) and crucial data are not published (e.g., first-measurement means on home practices; content of measures). Since both groups had identical outside reading assignments and true-false tests each week, and since the study discussion was didactic rather than non-directive, the design is not a fair contrast of lecture and discussion, as there is a third treatment applied to both groups, and the two major treatments are not very different.

Over all: (1) Course × attitudes and beliefs: +. (2) Course × practices: −.

WILNER, D. M., WALKLEY, R. P., PINKERTON, T. C., and TAYBACK, M. *The housing environment and family life: A longitudinal study of the effects of housing on morbidity and mental health.* Baltimore, Md.: Johns Hopkins Press, 1962.

Population: Low-income Negro families in Baltimore, Maryland, 1954–60.

Treatment: Moving into a new public housing project.

Dependent variables: Guttman attitude scales (typical items in parentheses): (*a*) Mood ("Do little things often make you feel blue?") (*b*) Control of temper ("Is it often hard for you to control your temper?") (*c*) Nervousness ("Are you a nervous person?") (*d*) Efficacy of self-help ("You can work hard and in the end you're back about where you started.") (*e*) Optimism ("There's no reason to believe that things are going to be a great deal better in the future.") (*f*) Satisfaction with personal state of affairs ("I'm really very happy about the way I've been getting along lately.")

Treatment groups: Data are reported for 300 experimentals admitted to public housing unit and 300 controls, matched on twenty-six social and housing characteristics; each group interviewed eleven times between April 9, 1955, and April 7, 1958, beginning prior to controls' acceptance by housing authority.

Results: As below, in terms of per cent in favorable half of dichotomized scales.

	Before		After		Net Change			Significant Difference E v. C After
	E	C	E	C	E	C	Difference	
Mood	37	37	56	52	+19	+15	+ 4	
Temper	46	47	47	45	+ 1	− 2	+ 3	
Nervousness	44	41	43	41	− 1	0	− 1	
Efficacy	49	43	53	46	+ 4	+ 4	0	
Optimism	39	36	48	39	+ 9	0	+ 9	> .05
Satisfaction	37	40	59	49	+22	+ 9	+13	> .05

Deficiencies: One of the best-designed and executed field experiments known to us. The authors note, however, that the controls
managed to better their housing considerably during the period
of the study; hence, the data may be assumed to underestimate
any effects of rehousing.

Over all: Although there are no clear-cut differences (compared, for
example, with the 38 per cent difference in "Net Change" for
the item "How do you like your apartment?"), the small trends
favor the experimentals more than the controls, and, as noted
above, the design probably underestimates effects. Miscellaneous
× subjective states: ?.

References

Some entries are annotated. All annotated entries are works cited in Chapters 2 and 3. Entries preceded by an asterisk (*) are experiments discussed in Chapter 4 and are treated more thoroughly in the Annotated Bibliography.

ANDERSON, J. E. *The young child in the home.* New York: D. Appleton-Century, 1936.

*ANDREW, G. A study of the effectiveness of a workshop method for mental health education. *Ment. Hygiene*, 1954, **38,** 627–33.

*ANDREW, G., SIBILIO, J. P., and STEHMAN, V. Utility of the small group discussion method as practiced in certain applied settings. 1. Instrumental goal achievement of a mental health group. *Amer. J. publ. Hlth,* 1960, **50,** 785–90.

*ASCH, M. J. Non-directive teaching in psychology: An experimental study. *Psychol. Monogr.,* 1951, Vol. **65** (No. 4).

BALDWIN, A. L., KALHORN, J., and BREESE, F. H. Patterns of parent behavior. *Psychol. Monogr.,* 1945, Vol. **58** (No. 3).

Intercorrelations and impressionistic interpretation of clusters of thirty rating scales (e.g., adjustment of the home, restrictiveness of regulations, child-centeredness of the home, coordination of the household) by a fieldworker who made twice-yearly visits to families of 150 children recruited from vicinity of Yellow Springs, Ohio, for participation in a longitudinal study.

*BALSER, B. H., BROWN, F., BROWN, M. L., JOSEPH, E. D., and PHILLIPS, D. K. Preliminary report on a controlled mental health workshop in a public school system. *Amer. J. Psychiat.,* 1955, **112,** 199–205.

*BALSER, B. H., BROWN, F., BROWN, M. L., and LASKI, L. Further report on experimental evaluation of mental hygiene techniques in school and community. *Amer. J. Psychiat.,* 1957, **113,** 733–39.

*BERKOWITZ, L. *Aggression: A social psychological analysis.* New York: McGraw-Hill Book Co., 1962.

BLOOD, R. O., JR., and WOLFE, D. M. *Husbands and wives: The dynamics of married living.* Glencoe, Ill.: Free Press, 1960.

Analysis correlates of role patterns and of marital adjustment based on personal interviews with a 1955 probability sample of Detroit wives aged twenty-one and over (N = 731) and a sample of 178 farm wives from three rural counties close to Detroit.

BLUM, R. H. Case identification in psychiatric epidemiology: Methods and problems. *Millbank Mem. Fund Quart.*, 1962, **40** (No. 3), 253 – 88.

A review and critique of research findings on psychiatrists' ratings and survey techniques in mental health research.

BOEK, W. E., LAWSON, E. D., YANKAUER, A., and SUSSMAN, M. B. *Social class, maternal health and child care.* Albany, N.Y.: New York State Department of Health, 1957.

Interviews with 1,432 new mothers sampled from birth certificates in areas near fifteen cooperating colleges in upstate New York. Provides data on mothers' usage of various books and pamphlets, as well as detailed tabulations of infant care and medical practices by mothers' class levels.

BOWLBY, J. *Maternal care and mental health.* Geneva: World Health Organization, 1951.

A review of a large number of clinical studies regarding the relationship between absence of the mother and mental health problems of young children. The author concludes that the evidence provides strong support for his proposition, but his conclusions are not universally accepted.

BREED, W., and KTSANES, T. Pluralistic ignorance in the process of opinion formation. *Publ. Opin. Quart.*, 1961, **25** (Fall) 382 – 92.

BRIM, O. G., Jr. *Education for child-rearing.* New York: Russell Sage Foundation, 1959.

A book-length review of research and problems in "parent education," concentrating on generalized assumptions and issues rather than detailed research findings.

BRONFENBRENNER, U. Socialization and social class through time and space. In E. E. MACCOBY, T. M. NEWCOMB, and E. L. HARTLEY (Eds.), *Readings in social psychology*. 3rd ed.; New York: Henry Holt and Co., 1958, pp. 400–425.

A detailed review and synthesis of fifteen studies of social class and child-rearing (from 1932 to 1957) with the general conclusion that class differences vary over time and essentially reflect differential influence by mass media and popular authorities.

*BRUCE, P. Relationship of self-acceptance to other variables with sixth-grade children oriented in self-understanding. *J. educ. Psychol.*, 1958, **49,** 229–38.

CAPLAN, G. *Prevention of mental disorders in children: Initial explorations*. New York: Basic Books, 1961.

Seventeen papers prepared by participants at a 1960 conference on prevention of mental disorders in children.

*CUMMING, E., and CUMMING, J. *Closed ranks: An experiment in mental health education*. Cambridge, Mass.: Harvard University Press, 1957.

CUMMING, E., and HENRY, W. E. *Growing old: The process of disengagement*. New York: Basic Books, 1961.

DAVIS, J. A. A formal interpretation of the theory of relative deprivation. *Sociometry,* 1959, **22,** 280–96.

———. Structural balance, mechanical solidarity, and interpersonal relations. *Amer. J. Sociol.*, 1963, **68** (January, No. 4), 444–62.

———. With D. GOTTLIEB, J. HAJDA, C. HUSON, and J. L. SPAETH. *Stipends and spouses: The finances of American arts and science graduate students*. Chicago: University of Chicago Press, 1962.

A survey of a national sample of 2,842 arts and science graduate students. Not a mental health study, but occasional data on adjustment are reported to compare effect of finances and other problems on student morale. Source of unpublished data treated in text of this volume.

ERSKINE, H. G. The polls: The informed public. *Publ. opin. Quart.*, 1962 (Winter), pp. 669–77.

FESTINGER, L. A theory of social comparison processes. *Hum. Relat.*, 1954, **7,** 117–40.

178

Education for Positive Mental Health

*FIEDLER, F. E. An experimental approach to preventive psychotherapy. *J. abnorm. and soc. Psychol.*, 1949, **44**, 386–93.
FIEDLER, F. E., DODGE, J. S., JONES, R. E., and HUTCHINS, E. B. Interrelations among measures of personality adjustment in nonclinical populations. *J. abnorm. and soc. Psychol.*, 1958, **56**, 345–51.

Intercorrelations of Taylor Anxiety Scale, semantic differential self-ratings, sociometric measures, health-center visits, etc., in two samples of college students (N = 87, 71) and two of soldiers (N = 52, 200).

FIEDLER, F. E., HUTCHINS, E. B., and DODGE, J. S. Quasi-therapeutic relations in small college and military groups. *Psychol. Monogr.*, 1959, **72**, 1–28.

Analysis of changes in mental health measures over time in the four samples described in the preceding reference. Concludes that "assumed similarity to others" is associated with improvement in mental health measures.

*FORD, M., and HARTMAN, E. E. Measuring reader comprehension of a preschool pamphlet. *Publ. hlth Reps.*, 1954, **69**, 498–502.
*GREENBERG, B. G., HARRIS, M. E., MacKINNON, C. F., and CHIPMAN, S. S. A method for evaluating the effectiveness of health education literature. *Amer. J. publ. Hlth*, 1953, **43**, 1147–55.
GURIN, G., VEROFF, J., and FELD, S. *Americans view their mental health.* New York: Basic Books, 1960.

Intercorrelations among, and correlations with, background variables for various subjective measures of mental health, based on a 1957 national area probability sample of 2,460 adults, aged twenty-one or older, living in private households.

HERZOG, E. *Some guide lines for evaluative research.* Washington, D.C.: U.S. Department of Health, Education, and Welfare, Social Security Administration, Children's Bureau, 1959.

Discussion and review of methodological techniques and issues with special emphasis on social-work evaluation; 345-item non-annotated bibliography.

HEYNS, R. W., and LIPPITT, R. Systematic observational techniques. In G. LINDZEY (Ed.), *Handbook of social psychology.* Vol. I: Reading, Mass.: Addison-Wesley Publishing Co., 1954, pp. 370–404.

HOLLINGSHEAD, A. B., and REDLICH, F. C. *Social class and mental illness: A çommunity study.* New York: John Wiley and Sons, 1958.

Rates for hospitalized and outpatient psychiatric treatment in New Haven, Connecticut, by social class, showing a strong negative association between class and hospitalized psychosis and a slight positive association between class and treated neurosis.

HUNTER, E. C. Changes in teachers' attitudes toward children's behavior over the last 30 years. *Ment. Hygiene,* 1957, **41,** 3–11.

Data on a 1955 study of New Orleans teachers' ratings of the seriousness of specific children's behavior problems, showing convergence toward ratings given by mental hygienists, as compared with Wickman's (1928) study.

INKELES, A. Industrial man: The relation of status to experience, perception, and value. *Amer. J. Sociol.,* 1960, **46** (July), 1–31.

A review of studies from a number of nations on the correlation between socio-economic status and personal adjustment.

JAHODA, M. *Current concepts of positive mental health.* New York: Basic Books, 1958.

A review and critique of a number of possible definitions and conceptualizations.

JANIS, I. *Psychological stress: Psychoanalytic and behavioral studies of surgical patients.* New York: John Wiley and Sons, 1958.

KELLY, J. G. *Community mental health and social psychiatry: A reference guide.* Cambridge, Mass.: Harvard University Press, 1962.

A non-annotated, 1,158-item bibliography on mental health (defined broadly) and mental health professions.

KENDALL, P. *Conflict and mood: Factors affecting stability of response.* Glencoe, Ill.: Free Press, 1954.

A technical study of determinants of stability of answers in longitudinal (panel) attitude surveys. Presents some data on continuity of "good spirits" in a large, although not representative, sample of 513 students from five universities.

KOTINSKY, R., and WITMER, H. (Eds.). *Community programs for mental health: Theory, practice, evaluation.* Cambridge, Mass.: Harvard University Press, 1955.

Seven essays on problems of conceptualizing mental health, descriptions of existing programs, and methodological problems of evaluation.

LANSING, J. B., and MORGAN, J. M. Consumer finances over the life cycle. In L. H. CLARK (Ed.), *Consumer behavior*, Vol. II. New York: New York University Press, 1955, pp. 36–51.

*LETON, D. A. An evaluation of group methods in mental hygiene. *Ment. Hygiene*, 1957, **41**, 525–33.

MACFARLANE, J. W. Study of personality development. In R. G. BARKER, J. S. KOUNIN, and H. F. WRIGHT (Eds.), *Child behavior and development: A course of representative studies.* New York: McGraw-Hill Book Co., 1943, Chap. 18, pp. 307–28.

A summary of the findings of the California Guidance Study described in the following citation.

MACFARLANE, J. W., ALLEN, L., and HONZIK, M. P. *A developmental study of the behavior problems of normal children between twenty-one months and fourteen years.* ("University of California Publications in Child Development," Vol. II.) Berkeley: University of California Press, 1954.

Longitudinal study of every third child born in Berkeley, California, between January 1, 1928, and June 30, 1929, utilizing physical examinations, psychological tests, and interviews with mothers. Sample divided into 126 experimentals provided with counseling services and 126 controls; samples matched on parental national derivation, income, father's occupation, SES, neighborhood, mother's age, and mother's education. Because of shrinkage, data at age fourteen are based on 41 mothers among controls compared with 16 at age ten, 91 at age five, and 116 at age one and three-fourths. Data reported in this volume concern time distribution, intercorrelations, and correlates of specific problems (e.g., "food finickiness," "diurnal enuresis," "specific fears," etc.).

*McGinnies, E., Lana, R., and Smith, C. The effects of sound films on opinions about mental illness in community discussion groups. *J. appl. Psychol.*, 1958, **42,** 40 – 46.

Merton, R., and Kitt, A. S. Contributions to the theory of reference group behavior. In R. K. Merton and P. F. Lazarsfeld (Eds.), *Continuities in social research.* Glencoe, Ill.: Free Press, 1950.

*Michigan State Department of Health. *A report of some aspects of the effectiveness of the Pierre the Pelican mental health pamphlets.* Lansing, Mich.: Michigan State Department of Health, 1952. (Mimeographed.)

Myers, R. C. Influence of age on physicians' views concerning mental health matters. *Publ. opin. Quart.*, 1955, pp. 252 – 58.

Schedules completed in fall, 1954, by 405 New Jersey physicians not specializing in psychiatry or neurology. Answers of those under fifty compared with answers of older practitioners. Younger physicians generally more interested in psychiatry, more aware of mental health problems, and had greater factual information.

*Nunnaly, J. C., Jr. *Popular conceptions of mental health: Their development and change.* New York: Holt, Rinehart, and Winston, 1961.

Reports of a large series of interrelated studies on experts' opinions on mental health topics, general-public opinions, content analyses of mass media, and experimental studies of the effect of various themes and techniques in mental health education. (Probably the single most important research project in mental health education.)

*Ojemann, R. H. Sources of infection revealed in preventive psychiatry research. *Amer. J. publ. Hlth*, 1960, **50,** 329 – 35.

O'Neal, P., and Robins, L. N. Childhood patterns predictive of adult schizophrenia: A 30-year follow-up study. *Amer. J. Psychiat.*, 1958, **114,** 385 – 91. (a)

(See Robins, Gyman, and O'Neal [1960] for a description of the study.) Reports a correlation between the number of symptoms given in case records of children referred to a guidance clinic and diagnosis in adulthood of schizophrenia. Based on 28 patients with adult diagnosis of schizophrenia and 107 patients diagnosed as having "no disease."

————. The relation of childhood behavior problems to adult psychiatric status: A 30-year follow-up of 150 subjects. *Ibid.*, pp. 961 – 69 (b)

(See Robins, Gyman, and O'Neal [1960] for a description of the study.) Reports data comparing adult adjustment of children referred to a child guidance clinic and control group matched from public school records. Patients, particularly those referred for delinquent or antisocial behavior, show lower levels of adult adjustment.

ORLANSKY, H. Infant care and personality. *Psychol. Bull.*, 1949, **46** (January), 1 – 48.

A review of the literature on relationships between infant-care practices and children's personality and adjustment. Concludes that no consistent correlations have been found. There are 149 references.

*OWINGS, C. *Studies in parental sex education.* Minneapolis, Minn.: University of Minneapolis Press, 1931.
PENNSYLVANIA MENTAL HEALTH, INC. *Mental health education: A critique.* Philadelphia: Pennsylvania Mental Health, Inc., 1960.

Summary of a 1958 conference and of background papers prepared for the conference. Raises questions which led to the commissioning of this volume.

PRESSEY, S. L., and KUHLEN, R. G. *Psychological development through the life span.* New York: Harper and Brothers, 1957.
*PRUGH, D. G., STAMB, E. M., SANDS, H. M., KIRSCHBAUM, R. M., and LENIHAN, E. A. A study of the emotional reactions of children and families to hospitalization and illness. *Amer. J. Orthopsychiat.*, 1953, **22**, 70 – 106.
RAMSEY, G., and SEIPP, M. Attitudes and opinions concerning mental illness. *Psychiat. Quart.*, 1948, **22**, 428 – 44.

Interviews with a quota sample (quotas set on sex, race, age, education, religion, occupation, and country of birth) of 345 respondents in Trenton, New Jersey. Tabulations by age, sex, education, occupation, separately for selected questions (e.g., "Do you or do you not think that insanity is inherited?" "Some people believe that poor living conditions are a cause of insanity. Others disagree. What is your opinion?"). General conclusion is that higher education is associated with more enlightened attitudes.

ROBINS, L. N., GYMAN, H., and O'NEAL, P. The interaction of social class and deviant behavior. *Amer. sociol. Rev.*, 1962, **27** (August), 480–92.

Adult occupational status of 524 children referred to a St. Louis municipal psychiatric clinic between 1924 and 1929, in contrast with 100 controls chosen from public school records. Concludes that patients have much less favorable occupational outcomes, but only patients referred because of antisocial behavior, neurotic and similar patients being no different from controls.

*ROGERS, J. M. Operant conditioning in a quasi-therapy setting. *J. abnorm. and soc. Psychol.*, 1960, **60**, 247–52.
*ROSE, A. M. Mental health attitudes of youth as influenced by a comic strip. *Journalism Quart.*, 1958, **35**, 333–42.
ROSENBERG, M. The dissonant religious context and emotional disturbance. *Amer. J. Sociol.*, 1962, **48** (July) 1–10.

Questionnaire data from approximately 1,000 public high-school juniors and seniors from ten high schools in New York State, apparently a representative probability sample. Students reporting themselves to be living in neighborhoods where the majority were of different religion during grammar school also report themselves lower on self-esteem, higher on psychosomatic symptoms and depressive affect.

ROTH, J., and PECK, R. F. Social class and social mobility factors related to marital adjustment. *Amer. sociol. Rev.*, 1951, **16** (August), 478–87.

A re-analysis of data on 523 cases in the Burgess and Cottrell marital-adjustment study, showing the relationship between the

Warner Index of Status Characteristics and the Burgess-Cottrell marriage-adjustment index.

*SCHAUS, H. S. An experimental investigation of methods in parent education. In K. W. HATTENDORF *et al.* (Eds.), *Researches in parent education. I.* ("University of Iowa Studies in Child Welfare," Vol. 6.) Iowa City, Iowa: University of Iowa, 1932, pp. 117–34.

SEARS, R. R., MACCOBY, E. E., and LEVIN, H. *Patterns of child rearing.* Evanston, Ill.: Row, Peterson and Co., 1957.

Studies of interrelations between child-rearing techniques and children's behavior, as reported by a sample of 379 mothers of kindergarten children in eight public schools in two suburbs of Boston.

SEWELL, W. H. Infant training and the personality of the child. *Amer. J. Sociol.*, 1952, **58**, 150–59.

Correlations between seven infant-care practices (e.g., breast-feeding versus bottle-feeding, early versus late bowel-training), as reported by mothers, and various measures of adjustment at ages five and six in a sample of 162 Wisconsin farm children. No reliable correlations were found.

SPOCK, B. *The pocket book of baby and child care.* New York: Pocket Books, Inc., 1946.

The single most influential source of doctrine on child development in contemporary America.

SROLE, L., LANGNER, T. S., MICHAEL, S. T., OPLER, M. K., and RENNIE, T. A. C. *Mental health in the metropolis.* New York: McGraw-Hill Book Co., 1962.

Demographic correlates (age, sex, marital status, socio-economic status, religion, ethnicity) of psychiatrists' ratings of mental health based on personal interviews with a probability sample of 1,660 respondents aged twenty to fifty-nine in a New York City neighborhood with a population of 175,000.

STAR, S. A. Psychoneurotic symptoms in the army. In S. A. STOUFFER *et al.*, *Studies in social psychology in World War II*. Vol. 2. Princeton, N. J.: Princeton University Press, 1949, pp. 411–55. (a)

Analysis of effects of overseas service and exposure to combat on Neuropsychiatric Screening Adjunct and on anxiety and psycho-somatic-symptoms indices constructed from NSA items. Based on self-administered questionnaires from large samples of soldiers in World War II.

————. The screening of psychoneurotics in the army: Technical development of tests. In S. A. STOUFFER *et al., Studies in social psychology in World War II.* Vol. 4. *Measurement and prediction.* Princeton, N. J.: Princeton University Press, 1949, pp. 486–547. (b)

A report on the development of a questionnaire designed to screen military inductees for evaluation by psychiatrists. Reports information on interrelations among a large number of predictors and on the differential ability of various predictors to discriminate between diagnosed neurotics and cross-sections within the army.

STONE, A. A., and ONQUE, G. C. *Longitudinal studies of child personality: Abstracts with index.* Cambridge, Mass.: Harvard University Press, 1959.

Abstracts of 297 longitudinal studies "primarily concerned with psychological [emotional and social] behavior" up to 1955.

STOUFFER, S. A. *Communism, conformity, and civil liberties.* New York: Doubleday and Co., 1955.

Report of personal interviews with a national sample of 4,939 adults and 1,500 community leaders, with data on political and personal worries; fieldwork completed in 1954.

STOUFFER, S. A., and DEVINNEY, L. C. How personal adjustment varied in the army. In S. A. STOUFFER *et al., Studies in social psychology in World War II.* Vol. 1. Princeton, N. J.: Princeton University Press, 1949, pp. 82–154.

Description of "personal esprit," "personal commitment," "satisfaction with status or job," and "approval or criticism of army" indices and patterns of association with age, education, marital status, longevity, etc. Based on self-administered questionnaires from large samples of soldiers in World War II.

STOUFFER, S. A., and OTHERS. *Studies in social psychology in World War II.* 4 vols. Vol. 1: *The American Soldier: Adjustment during army life;* Vol. 2: *The American soldier: Combat and its aftermath;* Vol. 3 (by C. I. HOVLAND, A. A. LUMSDAINE, and F. D. SHEFFIELD): *Experiments on mass communications;* Vol. 4: *Measurement and prediction.* Princeton, N.J.: Princeton University Press, 1949.

SUBCOMMITTEE ON EVALUATION OF MENTAL HEALTH ACTIVITIES, COMMUNITY SERVICES COMMITTEE, NATIONAL ADVISORY MENTAL HEALTH COUNCIL. *Evaluation in mental health: A review of the problem of evaluating mental health activities.* Washington, D.C.: U.S. Department of Health, Education, and Welfare, National Institute of Mental Health, 1956.

Discussion and recommendations regarding mental health evaluation research and 984-item annotated bibliography.

TAYLOR, J. A. A personality scale of manifest anxiety. *J. abnorm. and soc. Psychol.*, 1953, **48**, 285 – 90.

Description of the development of one of the most popular psychological self-rating scales. Items were selected from the Minnesota Multi-Phasic Inventory by judges on the basis of face validity, administered to samples of students, subjected to criterion of item-to-total correlations, and scale shown to distinguish between students and psychoneurotics in treatment. Sample items listed in text of this volume.

TERMAN, L. M., and ODEN, M. H. The gifted group at midlife. Stanford, Cal.: Stanford University Press, 1959.

VEROFF, J., FELD, S., and GURIN, G. Dimensions of subjective adjustment. *J. abnorm. and soc. Psychol.*, 1962, **64** (No. 3), 192 – 205.

Factor analysis of various subjective measures of mental health based on data of Gurin *et al.* (1960).

WICKMAN, E. K. *Children's behavior and teachers' attitudes.* New York: Commonwealth Fund, 1928.

Abstract reads, "It was found that schoolteachers were more concerned about overt violations of classroom routine than with fundamental behavior problems."

*WILNER, D. M., WALKLEY, R. P., PINKERTON, T. C., and TAYBACK, M. *The housing environment and family life: A longitudinal study of the effects of housing on morbidity and mental health.* Baltimore, Md.: Johns Hopkins University Press, 1962.

A longitudinal study contrasting the physical and mental health of three hundred lower-class Negro families in Baltimore, before and after entering public housing, with three hundred control families matched on a number of characteristics. Unpublished data on intercorrelations of mental health scales were kindly made available by Professor Wilner.

WOODWARD, J. L. Changing ideas on mental illness and its treatment. *Amer. sociol. Rev.*, 1951, **16**, 443–54.

Personal interviews with an area probability sample of 3,971 Louisville, Kentucky, residents aged eighteen and older; origins of mental illness, treatment of deviants, acceptance of psychiatry, etc., along with special samples of lawyers, doctors, teachers, and clergymen. Article reports tabulations by age and by education separately for a number of questions, e.g., "Suppose a member of your family became mentally ill. Do you think you would tell your friends and acquaintances about it?"

WOOTTON, B. Assisted by V. G. SEAL and R. CHAMBERS. *Social science and social pathology.* London: George Allen and Unwin, 1959.

An extensive review and critique of social-science knowledge regarding the causes of crime (with particular attention to Great Britain). Chapter 4, "Theories of the Effects of Maternal Separation or Deprivation," and Chapter 7, "Social Pathology and the Concepts of Mental Health and Mental Illness," are of particular interest in terms of the present document.

Index

Adult adjustment
  acceptance of principles of, 36–51
  correlation of acceptance of principles and, 62–63
  environmental correlates of, 63–98
    external events, 64–65
    demographic factors, 65–81
      age, 77–81
      sex, 65–68
      socio-economic status, 68–77
    social relationships, 81–98
      community differences, 81–83
      marital relationships, 83–88
      peer relationships, 88–95
      religion, 95–98
  past experiences and, 98–104
    age and, 77–81
Allen, L.; see MacFarlane et al.
American Soldier, The; see Star; Stouffer and DeVinney
Americans View Their Mental Health; see Gurin et al.
Anderson, J. E., 119
Andrew, G., 127
Andrew, G., et al. (1960), 135
Asch, M. J., 131

Baldwin, A. L., et al., 58, 59, 2.13
Balser, B. H., et al., 127, 128, 132
Berkowitz, L., 132
Bettelheim, B., 65–66
Blood, R. O., Jr., and Wolfe, D. M., 69, 77, 87, 88
Blum, R. H., 30
Boek, W. E., et al., 55
Bowlby, J., 111–13
Breed, W., and Ktsanes, T., 141
Breese, F. H.; see Baldwin et al.
Brim, O. G., Jr., 51, 107
Bronfenbrenner, U., 56–57
Brown, F.; see Balser et al.
Brown, M. L.; see Balser et al.
Bruce, P., 132

Child development
  acceptance of principles of, 51–55
  correlation of parental practices and parental beliefs, 56–59
  parental practices, 105–13
  parental mental health, 113–18
Chipman, S. S.; see Greenberg et al.
Community differences and adult adjustment, 81–83
Conclusions, 59–61, 118–22, 136–37, 138–52
Cumming, E., and Cumming, J., 128
Cumming, E., and Henry, W. E., 80

Davis, J. A., 92 n., 140 n.
  correlations of subjective measures, 20–21, 22
  environmental correlates of adult adjustment
    demographic factors (sex), 67, 68, 3.3
  social relationships
    marital relationships, 83–84
    peer relationships, 89–90
    religion, 97–98
Degree of mental health, 34–36
Demographic factors and adult adjustment, 65–81; see also Adult adjustment
DeVinney; see Stouffer and DeVinney
Dimensionality, 6–34
Dodge, J. S.; see Fiedler et al.

Environmental correlates of adult adjustment, 63–81; see also Adult adjustment
Erbe, W., 90
Erskine, H. G., 142 n.
Experimental studies, 123–37
  attitudes and beliefs, 126–31
  subjective states and practices, 131–36

NOTE: Numerals in *italics* are table numbers.

DATE DUE

MY 22 '69			
GAYLORD			PRINTED IN U.S.A.